Your Towns and Cities in the

Barnsley
in the Great War

*This book is dedicated to my uncles
Clifford Willoughby RAF,
Bomber Command (1920-2014)
and Stanley Nelder RN Submariner
(1923-2016)*

Your Towns and Cities in the Great War

Barnsley
in the Great War

Geoffrey Howse

Pen & Sword
MILITARY

First published in Great Britain in 2017 by
PEN & SWORD MILITARY
an imprint of
Pen and Sword Books Ltd
47 Church Street
Barnsley
South Yorkshire S70 2AS

Copyright © Geoffrey Howse, 2017

ISBN 978 1 47382 738 7

Printed and bound in England
by CPI Group (UK) Ltd, Croydon, CR0 4YY

Typeset in Times New Roman

Pen & Sword Books Ltd incorporates the imprints of
Pen & Sword Archaeology, Atlas, Aviation, Battleground, Discovery,
Family History, History, Maritime, Military, Naval, Politics, Railways,
Select, Social History, Transport, True Crime, and Claymore Press,
Frontline Books, Leo Cooper, Praetorian Press, Remember When,
Seaforth Publishing and Wharncliffe.

For a complete list of Pen and Sword titles please contact
Pen and Sword Books Limited
47 Church Street, Barnsley, South Yorkshire, S70 2AS, England
E-mail: enquiries@pen-and-sword.co.uk

Website: www.pen-and-sword.co.uk

Contents

Foreword

One hundred years ago, most families in Barnsley would have felt the pain and impact of the First World War on their lives, through the hardship and the loss or injury of loved ones. For the only time in our history, the Great War was very much a local war. Soldiers joined up en masse, and they trained and fought together. When a battle involving a local or regional battalion ended in tragedy, the community suffered as a whole.

My interest in Barnsley's Great War started over 40 years ago, when I rescued an album of photographs from a bonfire after sorting through some family keepsakes. Since then, I've gradually realised the importance and significance of these photographs to Barnsley, which provide unique insight into a war where we sent our bravest sons off to fight, many of whom did not return. Historians such as Jon Cooksey, Jane Ainsworth and now Geoffrey Howse in this book *Barnsley in The Great War* have pieced together this fascinating tale of optimistic recruitment which later gave way to sombre tragedy and loss.

The sons of Barnsley did us proud. They joined up in greater numbers than most towns and they fought in all of the major battles of the First World War, from Ypres to the Somme and Arras to Cambrai. This book is a fitting tribute to their memory.

Sir Nicholas Hewitt Bt

In July, 1919, a Mark IV 'female' tank was presented to the town on behalf of the National War Savings Committee. Here it is seen standing in Peel Square, before its journey to its eventual resting place in Locke Park.

Introduction

The long-term causes of the First World War can be traced back at least as early as the closing three decades of the nineteenth century. Broken alliances and German expansion caused considerable friction across Europe resulting in divisions which from 1882 were compounded by a gradual chain of events, eventually building up into an intolerable state of affairs. Tension reached a height between several European nations, especially in the troubled Balkan region, and the spark that ignited the tinder box finally occurred on 28 July 1914.

On 18 January 1871, Prussian statesman Otto von Bismarck (1815-1898) had succeeded in his ambition to unify Prussia and the German kingdoms into a single nation and had King Wilhelm I of Prussia proclaimed Kaiser of Germany. On 10 May 1871 France was forced to sign a humiliating treaty with Germany that ended the 1870-71 Franco-Prussian War. On 15 June 1888, Germany's first Kaiser died and was succeeded by his son Frederick III. Ninety-nine days later, on 15 June, Frederick III died and was succeeded by his 29-year-old son Wilhelm, who became King Wilhelm II of Prussia and Kaiser (Emperor) of Germany. 1888 became known as the Year of the Three Emperors.

In 1894, following the death of his father Alexander II, Tsar of Russia, on 1 November, his son Nicholas became Tsar Nicholas II. A friendship between Germany and Russia that had been in existence for some time was not renewed by the new Tsar and an adversarial relationship began between Russia and Germany. Friction, jealousy, avarice and distrust continued to be a major bone of contention among many of the European nations. In 1901, Queen Victoria of Great Britain and Empress of India, died on 22 January. Her bloodline ran through most of the royal ruling houses of Europe, which because of the esteem in which Her Majesty was held, in part had provided a degree of stability and served as a bond to hold many European nations in check.

On Queen Victoria's death her eldest son, Albert Edward, who had served as Prince of Wales for longer than any of his predecessors, acceded to the throne at the age of 59, as King Edward VII of the United Kingdom and the British Dominions and Emperor of India. The new king set about the modernisation of the British home fleet and of the British Army, after the Second Boer War (1899-1902).

Between 1904-05, the Russo-Japanese War resulted in a disastrous

HMS *Dreadnought*, launched in 1906.

defeat for Russia and caused major civil unrest at home. On 22 January 1905, the 'Bloody Sunday Massacre' by Tsarist troops in St Petersburg cost the Tsar support among the workers and farmers.

1906 saw the launch of the first British 'dreadnought'-class battleship. King Edward fostered good relations with other European countries, especially France, for which he was popularly referred to as a 'peacemaker'. His reign came at a time when changes in society and great strides in technology were taking place, on an unprecedented scale. However, despite his popularity elsewhere in Europe, the king's relationship with his nephew, Kaiser Wilhelm II was never good. He was a popular and greatly loved king, and the period in which he reigned, known as the Edwardian era, was named after him. At the time of his death on 6 May 1910, aged 68, he was embroiled in a constitutional crisis that was resolved by an Act of Parliament in 1911, which restricted the power of the House of Lords.

When Edward VII's second surviving son succeeded him as King George V, the new king found himself at the centre of the crisis that became known as the 'Budget Controversy'. Tories in the House of Lords rejected the budget proposed by the Liberal government in the House of Commons, they having considerably more peers than the government of the day. The king threatened to create enough new Liberal peers to pass the measure and the Tories gave in. The Parliament Bill was passed in 1911, without a mass creation of peers. That same year saw the king

Wilhelm II, the German
Kaiser and King of
Prussia from 1888 to
1918. He was the eldest
child of Crown Prince
Frederick of Prussia
and Victoria, daughter
of Queen Victoria.

King George V (right) closely resembled his cousin,
Tsar Nicholas II of Russia (left). Here they are seen in
German military uniforms in Berlin before the war.

visit India, the only king-emperor ever to have made the journey there.

King George V and his cousin Tsar Nicholas II, who were good friends, nurtured a dislike for their mutual cousin the Kaiser. This situation had existed since the three monarchs, who were all in a similar age group, were children.

Following the tragic events in Sarajevo on 28 June 1914, no small degree of uncertainty ensued as to what might next occur throughout Europe. Lloyd George, Chancellor of the Exchequer at the time of the assassination, recalled:

'I remember that sometime In July, an influential Hungarian lady called upon me at 11 Downing Street and told me that we were

During a visit to Yorkshire in 1912, King George V and Queen Mary inspected some of Barnsley's industrial centres and received a magnificent reception in the town centre. This is a commemorative postcard produced to mark the King and Queen's visit to Rylands glassworks.

The residents of Penistone line the streets for the visit of the King and Queen.

taking the assassination of the archduke much too quietly; that it had provoked such a storm throughout the Austrian Empire as she had never witnessed – and that unless something were done immediately, it would certainly result in war with Serbia, with the incalculable consequences which such an operation might precipitate in Europe. However, such official reports as came to hand did not seem to justify the alarmist view she took.'

The influential Hungarian lady's opinions were certainly based on firm foundations, as war was swift to follow.

King George became even more esteemed by his people during the First World War, when he made many visits overseas to the front line and to hospitals, factories and dockyards. In 1917, anti-German feeling prompted the king to change his family name to Windsor, abandoning the Germanic Saxe-Coburg-Gotha. When The Tsar was overthrown in the Russian Revolution of 1917, the British government offered him and his family political asylum. However, the plan by MI1 (British secret service) to rescue the Russian royal family was never implemented. Conflicting claims by Earl Mountbatten of Burma that it was the then Prime Minister David Lloyd George who opposed the plan and of Lord Stamfordham, that it was the king himself who opposed his government's idea, remains a matter of conjecture. The Tsar and his immediate family were killed by the Bolsheviks in 1918. The following year, the late Tsar's mother (King George's aunt) and other members of the extended Russian Imperial family, were rescued by British ships from the Crimea.

Before the First World War began, men as a general rule were thought of as 'breadwinners', bringing in the weekly wage, the majority of men undertaking gruelling and often tiring manual work. Only about 30 per cent of the workforce was female and the majority of unmarried working women were servants, others doing piecework at home. In the early 1900s there was a rise in the number of women taking office jobs and some women worked in factories or shops but it wasn't until the commencement of hostilities that dramatic changes took place. With so many men being out of the country fighting, women took on roles they had never imagined possible; although they were paid less than men, even when engaged in the same work, working women were better off than they ever had been. Many more women began to work in nursing and education during the war. Food prices in wartime Britain were high. In 1914 a family of four could be fed on £1 a week but by 1918 it was costing £2 a week and by that year there were five million women working in Britain.

The history of the First World War and the contribution made by the men of Barnsley and district directly involved in the conflict has been covered in depth in many other books and publications.

Throughout this book I have provided a timeline which makes reference to key events occurring during wartime and have included a variety of passages concerning a cross section of what was occurring on the home front in Barnsley and district while the war was raging abroad.

What the First World War was instrumental in changing throughout Great Britain was a wholesale act of levelling of the classes by the end of the conflict. Notwithstanding its sheer size, Yorkshire, in the present day, still has more manor houses, country mansions and stately homes (some of palatial proportions), per square mile than any other county, and Barnsley and District is blessed with a considerable number, despite the demolition of many fine country houses nationwide between the wars. After the First World War far fewer men and women were willing to enter service and during the decades that followed the number of those prepared to take on the role of domestic servants dwindled even further. The great houses no longer had large numbers of retainers, where in a few instances before the war, the higher servants, such as a household comptroller, or land agent, even had several of their own domestic staff, if they were not resident in the big house itself. The days when the local grocer, newsagent, butcher and ironmonger or the managers of department stores and the like, the more affluent of whom once had as many as three or more live-in servants, now found themselves with one at best, most having to make do with a charwoman.

Other important social changes benefiting everyone were instigated, in particular the need for greater control of public health and better housing for the working classes. The dramatic changes to the licensing laws regarding the supply and sale of liquor and beer had a profound effect on the working population during the war, many of the restrictions remaining in place until comparatively recent times; and I have included some interesting cases relating to these curious changes in the law, the penalties levied for infringement of which on analysis today seem disproportionately high.

I have only made reference to a tiny proportion of the horrendous number of industrial and agricultural casualties and deaths in Barnsley and district that took place between 1914-1918, but it must be remembered that a considerable number of members of the mining and metal working industries, and others not directly connected with the conflict, gave of their all to ensure victory.

Chapter One

Prelude to 'The War to End All Wars'

Barnsley and district lies amidst the largest of Yorkshire's ridings, in that southernmost portion of England's largest county by far, in a pocket of land within the West Riding, which has been traditionally referred to for several generations as South Yorkshire; with Barnsley and district most definitely being a major component of the beating heart of the great industrial West Riding.

The time between AD400 and 1066 was the most formative period of Yorkshire's history. During this period the area was settled by Saxon and Scandinavian people, when our language, our laws, church, weights and measures, system of government, coinage and our territorial boundaries were established. The Yorkshire Ridings came into being during this period. The term Riding is of Viking origin and derives from the Norse word Thrething, meaning a third. The East and North Ridings were separated by the River Derwent, and the West and North Ridings were separated by the River Ouse and the Ure – Nidd Watershed. The City of York itself was situated within all three Ridings. During the time that Yorkshire was under Norse domination the Ridings were further divided into areas known as wapentakes.

The town of Barnsley itself lies at the centre of the Staincross wapentake and was referred to as Berneslai in the Domesday Book of 1086, when the population was around 200. The town was in the parish of Silkstone and began to develop in the 1150s when what was at the time still a small village was given to Pontefract Priory. A market was established by Royal Charter in 1249. The monks made use of the geographical location of the village and developed a town nearby where three roads met: the Sheffield to Wakefield road, the Rotherham to Huddersfield Road and the old salt road via Saltersbrook, starting from Northwich in Cheshire and eventually passing through Barnsley to Doncaster. The original settlement became known as Old Barnsley and the town, which lies on the River Dearne gradually increased in size during the centuries that followed engulfing the original village within its extended boundaries.

During the seventeenth century Barnsley became a stopping off point for coaches travelling on the route between Leeds, Wakefield, Sheffield and onwards to London. Coaching inns became a feature of the town and trade increased as the population began to grow. By 1750 the town had a population of around 1,750 which rose between then and the census of 1811 to 5,014. The town became a major centre for linen weaving during the eighteenth and nineteenth centuries, when at the same time the rich coal and iron ore seams began to be exploited on an increasingly large scale. Barnsley also has a long tradition of glass making.

Farming continued to be a major employer of local labour along with associated trades prevalent throughout England but it was the introduction of heavy industry on a large scale that attracted new residents to Barnsley itself and the smaller towns and villages that fell within its district, many of which have older origins and richer histories than the town of Barnsley itself. Barnsley became a municipal borough in 1869, and a county borough in 1913.

The men of the area have played their part in the wars, battles and skirmishes that have taken place down the centuries. Much of this history has been covered in books and publications available for scrutiny in the excellent central and local public libraries and archives in Barnsley and district, and many are still available to purchase at the usual outlets; and, as the main focus of this book is to give the reader a taste of what was occurring throughout the area on the Home Front, during the period when what was generally believed to be at the time 'the war to end all wars,' I will end my brief introduction to the enormously rich, absorbing and fascinating history of this beautiful and historic area, concluding by summing up what has proven to be more of a blight than a blessing to Yorkshire in particular, and many other parts of England as a whole, whose cities, towns and smaller settlements suffered similar fates; when in 1974 during unwarranted local government changes throughout England, the Yorkshire Ridings were abolished, at least for administrative purposes, but not in the minds and hearts of the people of Yorkshire. The counties of North Yorkshire, West Yorkshire and South Yorkshire were created, as were Cleveland and Humberside, which took away historic parts of Yorkshire. Fortunately, Cleveland and Humberside have themselves been abolished and returned to Yorkshire. So at the present time Yorkshire is today referred to as North, West and South Yorkshire.

From 1974, the new county of South Yorkshire incorporated the newly created metropolitan boroughs of Barnsley, Doncaster, Rotherham and

Sheffield, with Barnsley being chosen as the administrative headquarters of the South Yorkshire County Council, created on 1 April 1974, from thirty-two local government districts of the West Riding and four independent county boroughs, as well as small areas from Derbyshire and Nottinghamshire. South Yorkshire County Council along with all the other metropolitan county councils throughout England was abolished in 1986; but the four metropolitan boroughs remain, at least in name form, although they are effectively unitary authorities. In the present day, as a ceremonial county, South Yorkshire has a Lord Lieutenant and a High Sheriff. The once, more independently governed urban district councils and rural district councils that administered and looked after what is referred to by many as 'Gods own Country', generally meaning the county of Yorkshire as it was until the last quarter of the twentieth century, were swept away in 1974. Recently, the town of Barnsley itself has been undergoing major development and a programme of urban improvement, as have some of its satellite towns, and villages, including Grimethorpe and Hoyland, which will help to create more employment opportunities and a strong indication that greater prosperity will soon return to the area, helping to fill the void that has existed largely since 1984, when the closure of the area's coal mines and heavy industries began.

The rich history of Barnsley and district is gradually been exploited and tourism is on the increase. The sacrifices made by the gallant men and women of Barnsley in the First World War or the 'Great War' as this horrendous conflict is often referred to, should never be forgotten; but while many of the fittest men were fighting at land, sea and later in the air; others were playing their part at home and women took on roles they had never imagined would have been possible. The optimism that was prevalent at the beginning of George V's reign was shortly to be blighted. Many brave men lost their lives throughout the area or suffered terrible injuries, both physical and psychological. Some were honoured for their exceptional acts of bravery over and above the call of duty. The loss of such a vast number of men during the conflict resulted in many young women in the area never marrying, such was the scarcity of suitable beaux. Indeed, three of my grandfather's five sisters, who lived in Elsecar, lost their betrothed during the conflict, and throughout their long lives, never married. The First World War had long-term consequences for considerable numbers of our community. The sacrifices that were made by so many should never be forgotten.

The bustling market in May Day Green during the early 1900s. The Cross Keys Hotel can just be seen on the right of the photograph. Tasker Trust

Chapter Two

1914: Storm Clouds Gather

The burst of optimism that had been generated throughout England in 1913, fuelled by an increase in trade, had spilled over into 1914. The 50,000 inhabitants of Barnsley were given every reason to be confident that their circumstances would continue to improve, as they had done during the previous year. The wheels of industry were turning at an ever increasing rate and the demand for coal continued to provide regular employment for a large body of men working underground throughout the area, notwithstanding the mining support industries that provided a goodly supply of diverse working opportunities for the surface workers in that industry. Local tradesmen and women had been busy in the months leading up to the festive season; and were continuing at a healthy pace in the New Year. Barnsley Post Office reported that a record had been established in the lead up to Christmas and described their staff as being 'simply swamped with work'. The postmaster reported that an unprecedented number of deliveries of parcels, packages, letters, cards and postcards had been made in the days leading up to Christmas Day, and there was another heavy rush on New Year's Day.

That feeling of optimism remained as winter turned into spring and

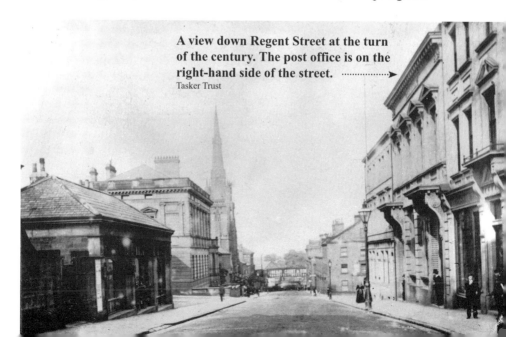

A view down Regent Street at the turn of the century. The post office is on the right-hand side of the street. ⋯⋯⋯➤
Tasker Trust

Franz Ferdinand and his wife, Sophie, leave the town hall for a tour of Sarajevo in an open-topped car as one of a motorcade of five cars. Six conspirators lined the route along the Appel Quay, each one with instructions to try to kill Franz Ferdinand when the royal car reached his position. The first conspirator lost his nerve. Then a student member of the gang threw a hand grenade at the Archduke's car which exploded under the wheel of the fourth car wounding two of the occupants. Franz Ferdinand decided to go to the hospital and visit the injured. On the way there the driver took a right turn into Franz Josef Street. Princip was standing near Moritz Schiller's cafe when Franz Ferdinand's car stopped, having taken the wrong turn. Upon realizing his mistake, the driver braked, and began to reverse giving Princip his opportunity. At a distance of about five feet Princip shot Franz Ferdinand in the neck and Sophie in the abdomen. They were both dead before 11.00 am.

spring turned into summer. It was at the very end of that first week of summer 1914 that an act of violence far from Britain's shores, the small, little known Balkan country, then known as Servia (now known as Serbia) triggered a series of events that within a little over five weeks would see Great Britain at war.

The people of Great Britain were oblivious to quite how their lives would be affected by conflict on such an unprecedented scale. Having been at peace with Europe for a century nobody had experienced anything like it. The entire nation was shortly in for a massive shock, when the horror and reality of modern warfare reared its ugly head.

While the events at the end of the previous month in Sarajevo had certainly been taken notice of in the country as a whole, no alarm bells had been quick to ring in the ears of the vast majority of the general public. The political complexities that spanned some parts of Europe were of no apparent concern to the ordinary man in the street; and indeed, life in Barnsley and district carried on as it did in other parts of Great Britain at its usual steady pace.

Some concern was expressed locally that the summer heat and the inadequate rainfall in the earlier months of the year was the reason given for various parts of Yorkshire experiencing a serious shortage in the water supply during the first weeks of July. This was particularly prevalent in some parts of the South Yorkshire colliery district, where housing questions and the cognate problems of sanitation were pressing for a speedy solution. Concerns were expressed that public health could not be easily maintained without a pure and copious supply of water. The *Barnsley Chronicle* in its 11 July edition commented that 'The supply from Midhope and Ingbirchworth is quite adequate to the requirements of the Borough; and Barnsley's future wants are also wisely provided for; thanks to the forethought of the Town Council.' The correspondent went on to say that in contrast to this satisfactory outlook in the case of the Borough, some of the rural districts in other parts of Yorkshire seemed likely to be confronted with something like a water famine.

In the same edition concerns were raised about the regrettable fact that the Yorkshire Territorials would go into camp that summer very seriously below their establishment strength. It transpired at a recent meeting of the West Riding Association, that there was in the Division a deficiency of 3,000 men; one Brigade being sixteen officers and 1,500 men short. Comments were made concerning the fact that Barnsley was always a popular recruiting centre for the Old Volunteer corps, and at

---

June 1914
28th
Austrian Archduke Franz Ferdinand, heir to the Austro-Hungarian throne, was assassinated at Sarajevo along with his wife Archduchess Sophie, by a Bosnian Serb student, 19-year-old, Gavrilo Princip. Franz Ferdinand's death was the spark that ignited the First World War.

July 1914
5th
Kaiser Wilhelm II promised German support for Austria against Serbia.
14th
Austro-Hungarian Ministers finally determined a strategy of action against Serbia.
19th
Council of Austro-Hungarian Ministers approved a draft of ultimatum to Serbia.
23rd
Austro-Hungarian Government sent ultimatum to Serbia.

Territorial headquarters at Eastgate, the centre of activity in August 1914.

the supreme crisis during the Boer War, Barnsley, to its imperishable honour, sent numbers of its sons to the front. Brave and patriotic men who at duty's call sprang gallantly into the fighting line. It was also stated that it was right at such a juncture to recall to the young men of today the magnificent deeds done by Barnsley's 'warriors' in the not remote past. Courageous men, who nobly volunteered for active service, and who when the bullets were flying the thickest, valiantly maintained the 'dogged fighting qualities of the British Race'. These men of Barnsley showed that their patriotism was indeed a reality.

Further comments were expressed concerning the civil defence of the nation and the question was asked: Will Barnsley's sons now be less responsive to the country's call for men to fill the depleted ranks of the Army of The Home Defence? – a trained force of citizen soldiers who constitute for the country's hearths and homes, a true National Guard.

There was great excitement in Barnsley on the afternoon of Tuesday, 21 July at the opening of the new public baths The new baths were formally opened by Alderman Henry Holden, Chairman of the Sanitary Committee. In respect of the views only recently expressed at the

The new Race Street public baths, just off York Street, were opened 21 July, 1914. Old Barnsley

Alderman Henry Holden formally opened the baths.

general shortage of water in parts of Yorkshire, many a wry smile was noted during the proceedings and several jocular remarks were passed around the assembled company, with the resultant 'Chinese whispering' effect, originally emanating from the lips of some of the areas more inventive wags, and provided no small degree of amusement among some of those present as the inevitable jokes were passed around.

In the evening, Alderman Holden was entertained by the council to a complimentary dinner at the Queen's Hotel, and a company of about twenty members of the council and principal officials sat down to an excellent repast.

Despite the summer temperatures, much was made of by certain ladies in the town and district of the coming fashions – designs and patterns of beautiful dresses by Madame Gwendolen Hope. Also some attention

was given to the protection of what, to many discerning local ladies of fashion, might arguably be their most valuable items of attire. Indeed, it was expressed in print in mid-July that 'Now is the time to buy one's furs for the coming winter, if one has not already got a set ... Now, too, is the time to have our treasures remodelled. If we think that process necessary, before the furriers get busy with their winter orders; and the prices charged out of season at nothing like as high as later on, when the "hands" are up to their eyes in work. An excellent plan for keeping moths away just now, which is their most mischievous period, if we are brave enough to keep our furs at home, is to cover them with tissue paper, then with newspaper, and hermetically seal them by pasting down the edges and allowing them to dry before putting away. Some people put bunches of dry mint in the drawers or boxes with their furs.'

> **August 1914**
> **1st**
> Germany declared war on Russia.
> **3rd**
> Germany declared war on France and invaded Belgium.
> **4th**
> Britain declares war on Germany.

On 3 August, a scorching Bank Holiday Monday, as tension mounted all day long, a packed House of Commons debated whether Britain should remain neutral in the crisis. Lord Kitchener, hero of the skirmishes in the Sudan, was recalled to London for an appointment at the War Office.

Four days after declaration of war the Defence of the Realm Act was passed in England (commonly referred to as DORA), which allowed the government to prosecute anyone whose actions were deemed to 'jeopardise the success of His Majesty's forces or to assist the enemy'. As the war progressed new restrictions were added to the Act, widening its scope to give further protection against a whole range of activities deemed to present possible threats to security or the well-being of the nation.

On Saturday, 8 August the *Barnsley Chronicle* reported:

'Germany having taken the final tragic plunge, the war cloud which for some time past threatened Europe has burst and the country is plunged into what promises to be THE greatest war which has ever occurred. On Saturday night the German Ambassador, in the name of his government, handed to the Foreign Ministry a declaration of War upon France, and on Tuesday took the same dramatic step with England.

'The week has been one series of exciting events. Here in Barnsley, like other towns, the gravest concern has been displayed on all hands, and the Reservists, Territorials, and other patriotic townsmen have willingly offered their services to their King and country.

'The 'Signing on' process has been going on all week, and it is no exaggeration to say that the loyalty displayed has even eclipsed that shown when war was declared with South Africa.'

Field Marshal Earl Kitchener (1850-1916), hero of the Sudan, and Secretary of State for War. He played a significant part in recruitment for the war. Lord Kitchener drowned on 5 June 1916, along with over 600 men, who were on board HMS *Hampshire* when it was struck by a German mine off the Orkney Islands.

The war that was now already raging in Europe in its early stages began quite suddenly out of the murder of the Austrian Archduke Franz Ferdinand, and his wife. Austria regarded this murder of her prospective Emperor as the work of Serbia, and called upon that country to carry out several acts of reparation. At first Serbia seemed inclined to give way, but owing as it was thought, to the influence of Russia, she eventually refused to do what was asked of her. Austria then declared war and began to bombard Belgrade, the chief seat of the Serbians, who withdrew their court and government, because it was thought that the city could not long be defended.

Concerns were raised about the balance of power in Europe. Some years previously, Germany, Austria and Italy entered into an agreement known as the Triple Alliance. France and Russia did not like this so they entered into a similar alliance.

During the reign of Edward VII, Britain strove to court better relations with France. Thanks in no part to the unstinting efforts of His Majesty and to the delight of His Majesty's government and subjects, the Entente Cordiale came into being. Through this, relations with Russia began to improve, so that the Triple Alliance came to be balanced by the Triple Entente. When Austria went to war with Serbia Russia objected, because the Russians were of a similar race to the Serbians and regarded them as under their guidance. As Austria did not desist from their attack on Belgrade, Russia prepared to go to war on Serbia's behalf. Then because Austria was affected, Germany, her ally, entered the fray, and at once made war on Russia, and on France as Russia's ally.

Italy at first stood aloof from the rapidly escalating proceedings. Having sided with Germany and Austro-Hungary in the Triple Alliance, in theory it was not only presumed but expected that she would naturally join forces with her allies. Instead, Italy chose to wait and see how the war progressed. Having taken quite some time to evaluate the situation, she finally turned against her allies and after a wait of over nine months, she entered war on the side of the Triple Entente on 23 May 1915.

During the week leading up to Thursday, 6 August, Barnsley Drill Hall was the centre of great interest and activity, and the frequent appearances in the streets of members of the local Territorial detachment in service dress made the inhabitants of Barnsley realise how near the war was to them. The Barnsley detachment of the 5th Battalion of the York and Lancaster Regiment was, in common with other units of the Territorial Army recalled from the annual training camp at Whitby on the Monday of that week, and on their arrival at Barnsley were looking very fit. Only one of the two-weeks training had been completed and some of the men had only been at the camp for 24 hours. The men, knowing fully the crisis through which the country was passing, eagerly awaited developments. These were soon forthcoming and within a short time of the receipt of the 'Royal Proclamation for the embodying of the Territorials', on Tuesday evening, notices were posted all over the town. As the news became known, great numbers of people turned out to watch the proceedings, and the war appeared to be the sole topic of conversation. Little groups of people eagerly discussed the situation, and there was naturally a big crowd in the vicinity of the Drill Hall.

The Territorials upon their dismissal after their premature return from camp, were fully appraised as to what might happen, and what their duties would be in that case. The proclamation therefore, did not come as a surprise. The Territorials were fully prepared for the eventuality, it was greatly to the credit of the Barnsley citizen soldiers that they so quickly reported themselves at their headquarters. On Tuesday night a rumour was current in the town that the Barnsley detachment would leave at midnight, and many persons waited about for the purpose of seeing their departure. As a matter of fact, of course, neither the officers nor the men knew when nor where they were going. All they could do was to obey orders and hold themselves in readiness. During Wednesday it became known that the detachment would leave the town on Thursday afternoon, and the men were busy all day making the final preparations. The Territorial Army had a total force of in excess of 207,700 men, with the Barnsley contingent numbering 220.

On Wednesday, the officers of the detachment travelled to Rotherham (the headquarters of the battalion), where they received their orders, and upon their return to Barnsley it was definitely announced that the first move from the local barracks would be made on Thursday, the destination being Rotherham, where the men were quartered in schools and other suitable buildings pending further orders.

The excitement reached its climax on Thursday, when the detachment left by Midland train for Rotherham at 3.30 in the afternoon. Throughout the morning great anticipation prevailed in the town, a big crowd gathering in the vicinity of the Drill Hall. During the morning the men were paraded for medical examination and inspection of kit.

The men were given a civic send off. This took place on Market Hill in the early afternoon, and a scene of the greatest enthusiasm took place, in which many of the assembled crowd commented that it was an occasion that would be long remembered in the history of Barnsley. A huge but well-behaved crowd gathered in Market Hill and vicinity, and at 2.30 pm the Mayor of Barnsley (Councillor W.G. England), in full robes and chain of office, with the Mayoress, the Town Clerk and most of the members and officials of the Town Council, walked in procession from the Town Hall, the mayor proceeded by constables bearing the mace and banner of the town. They waited on the steps of the Corn Exchange for the commander of the 5th Batallion York and Lancaster Regiment, Lieutenant-Colonel Fox. Two companies of infantry, signalling and ambulance corps, numbering in all about 200, marched into the centre of Market Hill and paraded. Their appearance was very smart, and many

**The first wartime civic send-off for Barnsley soldiers. The Mayor of
Barnsley, Councillor England and other dignitaries await the arrival of
the Territorials on Market Hill.**

expressions of approval were heard. The men, who carried their rifles,
and were equipped for marching, looked eager and fit.

In addressing the assembled body of men the mayor told them:

*'On behalf of the citizens of this town, and speaking with a full
sense of the responsibilities which rest upon me on this momentous
occasion, I have come to wish you God-speed on the mission
you have undertaken. The cloud which for forty years has been
gathering over our heads has suddenly burst, and we as a nation
are compelled to go into war that has been forced upon us by the
mad caprice of the German Emperor. But we know we are standing*

for the defence of the weak, the champions of the liberties of countries that for years have enjoyed our friendship and support. [The mayor's speech was at this point interrupted with loud cries of "Hear Hear"] *The marvellous manner in which the mobilisation of the forces has been accomplished, must have been an object lesson to the nations around us, for never in the history of our nation have our naval and military forces been ready at such short notice. The call has been made, and it has instantly and willingly been obeyed. For some years you have played your part as citizens, but now at short notice you are soldiers of the King. See to it you acquit yourselves like men.* [More loud cries of "Hear Hear" were uttered]. *And to quote* The Times *of the other day, in this hour of national trial go into it united, calm, resolute, trusting in God –*

Colonel Fox and his 'weekend soldiers' parade on Market Hill, before leaving for regimental headquarters at Rotherham.

that is the mood in which our fathers fought in the firm hope that in a just and righteous cause, the only giver of all victory will bless our army. On behalf of our townsmen I sincerely wish you God-speed, and a safe and speedy return to your native town.'

The conclusion of the moving speech was met with thunderous applause.

The detachment then marched directly via Eldon Street from Market Hill to the Midland Railway Station, where a big crowd of friends and relatives saw them off. It was noticed that the men seemed in the best of spirits and were delighted with the reception that had been given them.

Concerns were expressed locally about possible disruption to food supplies; reassuring statements were soon forthcoming in local newspapers, one in the *Barnsley Chronicle* stated:

'At this crisis in our country's history, the quality and the quantity of the harvest is of supreme importance to our people. It is therefore, good news to learn that the wheat crop is very satisfactory, barley, too, is an excellent crop, while potatoes are exceptionally abundant ... Fortunately there is plenty of produce in the country. Now that the home harvest is rapidly nearing completion, sufficient wheat will be at hand until the arrival of the grain ships from America and other parts ... Quite sure we are that Barnsley, for its part, will do its duty as splendidly as its citizen soldiers are doing theirs. It will be remembered how our patriotic fund afforded sustained and invaluable succour to the families of Barnsley soldiers at the time of the South African War. As intimated in our columns last week this fund has been revived to meet the present supreme emergency. It should be noted that those eligible for assistance from its funds will be the dependants of the Territorials belonging to the Barnsley Detachment, and the County Borough of Barnsley's Reservists ... Barnsley generosity has never yet failed in a good cause, and we are confident that it is not going to fail now. Barnsley hearts and Barnsley sympathies are with her brave lads who promptly sprang to arms in their country's cause. To provide for these men's wives and families is a sacred trust and a patriotic privilege ... All can help. The wealthy can give of their abundance, and other people according to their means. Now is the time for all classes to pull together, and to show to the world that the true British spirit survives in all its pristine power – a spirit that shall preserve our liberties inviolate and safeguard our shores from foreign aggression, a spirit which shall impel us to chivalrously rush to

the defence of Belgium and any other small nation threatened by the tyranny of the Teuton, a spirit which shall win for our country fresh laurels and new triumphs, for true, indeed, is it that – Not once not twice in our dear island story, The Path of Duty was the way to Glory!'

On Saturday, 15 August, the sixteenth annual show in connection with the Ardsley Allotment and Cottage Gardening Society was held in the Ardsley Working Men's Club and Institute, the show being the most successful in the society's history; and on the following Thursday, the 56th annual agricultural show took place at Penistone, under the auspices of the Penistone Agricultural, Horticultural and Floral Society. The weather was excellent and despite the national crisis, the attendance was well up to the average. During that week at the Pavilion cinema in Barnsley, the star turn was provided by Fred Ryedale and his dainty little ladies, who were to be seen in *Fun in a Houseboat*, with pretty illuminated scenes. Patrons of the Pavilion were reminded that they may rely on seeing war pictures as soon as the censor permitted them to be shown. At the Princess Picture Palace a popular feature was a film entitled *Europe in Arms*.

On the evening of Russia's unfortunate defeats, Hoyland Nether Urban District Council convened a meeting of townspeople in the Town Hall, to form a committee to deal with distress in consequence of the war. The Chairman of the Council, Nathanial Mell, presided. By a small majority it was decided to send the whole of the money raised in the district to the National Fund. Although there was a fairly large attendance, the chairman expressed the opinion that he was a bit disappointed that the gathering was not even greater as the subject they had met to discuss was a very important one indeed. At Monk Bretton on the previous Saturday the Monk Bretton Patriotic Fund had done some good work locally, when thirteen soldier's wives and twenty-four children were relieved, each woman receiving £1 and each child 2s. At Mapplewell and Staincross a large committee of ladies was formed as a branch of the Red Cross Guild. Immediately active, a series of meetings were quickly arranged for sewing sessions and a parcel of bandages, shirts, socks etc., was

August 1914
12th
The British Expeditionary Force started its retreat from Mons. Germany declared war on France.

26th
The Russian army was defeated at Tannenburg and the Masurian Lakes.

shortly forwarded to Queen Mary's distribution agency. Members of the Guild were reported to be very busy.

September 1914

On the afternoon of the first day of the month there was great excitement as the new baths erected over the previous twelve months or so at a cost of £7,400, were opened in Wombwell's Hough Lane. The event attracted a crowd of about 700 people. Within the extensive buildings, in addition to the large swimming bath, there was also a smaller swimming pool intended for children or those wishing to learn to swim; and twelve slipper baths (eight for gentlemen and four for ladies). In addition there was also a laundry, and moreover, the manager and manageress of the impressive new baths lived on the premises.

> **September 1914**
> **6th**
> The Battle of Marne began.

On the same Sunday as the battle at Marne began, a splendid concert was held in the evening at the Barnsley Empire in aid of the Barnsley Patriotic Fund, making it possible to hand over the impressive sum of £44.3s. 4d. at the end of the performance.

On Tuesday, 8 September a meeting described as probably the largest ever held in Penistone took place in a large shed adjacent to the Rose and Crown. Mr Sydney Arnold, MP for the division was in the chair, and with him were the Right Hon the Earl of Wharncliffe, some local notables and members of Penistone Urban District Council, the purpose being to establish a Distress Fund in Penistone. Mr Arnold said that he felt a great responsibility, one from which he could not shirk... Seven nations of Europe were engaged in the most strenuous war the world had ever seen and it was the bounded duty of every countryman and woman to put forth every effort to bring the war to a speedy and successful

Wortley Hall, the seat of the Earl of Wharncliffe.

conclusion. Mr Arnold urged the assembled crowd to think of the horrors of invasion. Belgium had been used because it was a short cut to France … The House of Commons had passed an address pledging the country to Support Belgium to the end: 'But it was not only for Belgium that we were fighting. We were fighting for our own sakes; our lives. Our gallant little Army at the front had fought nobly. It had worthily maintained its traditions.' It was our duty to send out more men, and he believed they would be forthcoming. Lord Wharncliffe, speaking with great dignity and passion, said he had made it a condition of his coming to the meeting that both parties should be represented. There was only one political party at present – the British – and only one policy. They had all heard of the atrocities which had been committed in the name of 'justice'. His Lordship warned those meeting what the effects of the Germans winning the war would be, the crushing indemnity, and the occupation of the country. He said the colonies had done grandly, and asked the question, to which was suspected his Lordship already knew the answer, were we, the mother country, going to be put to shame by our children of the colonies?

Lieutenant-Colonel Hodgekinson proposed a vote of thanks to the chairman and his Lordship, which Dr A. C. Wilson seconded and Mr J. M. Spencer-Stanhope (of Cannon Hall, Cawthorne) seconded. Afterwards, recruiting for the newly-established Distress Fund proceeded at a brisk rate.

On the afternoon of 23 September a representative gathering of ladies at Barnsley Town Hall instituted another splendid movement for the lessening of distress caused by the war and received an encouraging start. It was decided to form a committee to support the Queen Mary's Work for Women scheme. The mayoress (Mrs W.G. England), convened the meeting, attended by about seventy women.

The queen had formed a central committee to obtain funds in the first instance to assist her to provide work for women cast out of employment by reason of the war. In Barnsley that had occurred in several instances. At the Prince of Wales' Fund meeting held on the previous day it was established that the greater portion of the distress relieved was from one firm in Barnsley, and that firm mostly employed women. The mayoress said that this fund, being discussed by them presently, however, was not for the purpose of paying money to women who were cast out of employment, but to provide work for those women, because the queen had the right feeling, which probably she always had, to know that women did not wish for charity, but they wanted the right to be employed and the rights to receive the fruits of their employment. The queen had formed this committee and she had asked the mayoress to get funds to send to the central fund. They would then have to find out where unemployment occurred by reason of the war, and to report that unemployment, and to report also, or suggest, what in their opinion would be the best means of finding employment, or what employment would be the best to be provided for these women. Resources would then be directed as appropriate to individual circumstances. Unlike some other places in Yorkshire (including Bradford, where 2,000 khaki uniforms had been directed to be made, providing employment for women) female work in Barnsley, as yet, had not become acute. And new opportunities for the employment of women would soon present themselves. Collecting cards for Queen Mary's Work for Women were then distributed, with instructions that these be returned to Mrs Hewitt, hon treasurer, at Ouslethwaite Hall, Worsbrough.

During the last week of September recruitment for the Barnsley battalion had been very successful. Colonel Hewitt and his officers expressed confidence that the full complement of men would soon be forthcoming.

October 1914

On Saturday, 3 October, it was 'Emblem Day' at Hoyland, and throughout the day young ladies, under the direction of the Reverend H.T. Clark, were selling emblems, the proceeds of which were for the Patriotic Fund. The Hoyland town, Rockingham colliery and Elsecar brass bands, paraded the streets playing national airs. The sum of £77 was realised.

It was noted with great appreciation that encouraging efforts were being made by the ladies of the village of Carlton to assist the Patriotic Fund. In addition to raising £17 at a garden party held at the vicarage (this amount being handed to the Belgian Consul at Leeds), current efforts were being directed at helping the Lundwood Hospital, in the shape of shirts and socks for use by the wounded soldiers. Money raised from regular local collections was used to purchase materials to supply the shirts and socks, there being no lack of eager sewers and knitters.

> **October 1914**
> **18th**
> The First Battle of Ypres.
> **29th**
> Turkey entered the war on Germany's side.

In the Saturday, 24 October edition of the *Barnsley Chronicle* it was reported that Mrs W.K. Peace of Green Bank, Thurgoland, whose husband was serving at the front, some time intimated to the authorities that she was prepared to take some wounded soldiers, and on the evening of Tuesday, 20 October she had the pleasure of receiving a soldier who had that day travelled from Netley Hospital. The soldier concerned had been engaged in the battle at Mons, where on 26 August a shrapnel bullet entered

British infantry manning some defence positions in the Ypres Salient during the First Battle of Ypres.

November 1914

1st

The First Battle of Ypres. Great Britain and Turkey commenced hostilities.

During naval action off Cornel, HMS *Good Hope* and HMS *Monmouth* were sunk by Admiral von Spee's Squadron.

Russia declared war on Turkey.

A 'State of War' commenced between Serbia and Turkey.

The British Admiralty declared the North Sea a military zone.

3rd

The first German naval raid on the British coast took place near Gorleston and Yarmouth.

Allied squadrons bombarded forts at the entrance to the Dardanelles.

5th

Great Britain and France formally declared war on Turkey.

The British submarine *B-11* proceeded two miles up the Dardanelles (this being the first warship to enter the straits).

11th

The Battle of Nonneboschen (Ypres). An attack by the German Guard was repulsed.

HMS *Niger* was sunk by a German submarine off Deal.

12th

Orders were issued for all British aeroplanes on the Western Front to bear distinguishing marks.

22nd

The Battles of Ypres, 1914 ended.

his knee. The soldier was expected to join the depot at Pontefract after a further two weeks recuperation. It was expressed that example might be followed by others who desired to render such service to their King and Country.

November 1914

On Wednesday, 4 November an evening lecture on 'How Germany Makes War', illustrated by eighty slides, was given in the National Schoolroom at Thurgoland. The proceeds of the well-attended and most interesting event being in aid of the National Relief Fund; and on Friday evening, a meeting of the War Distress Fund Committee was held, when it was arranged to provide for a family of Belgian Refugees at an empty house in the centre of the village.

When the war broke out the Yorkshire glass-bottle trade received a serious check, notwithstanding that within Barnsley itself; since then, much to the relief of those locally employed in this long-established industry, business has recovered to some extent. Recent enquiries began coming in from sources which had hitherto looked to the continent for their supplies and manufacturers hopes were raised that some portion of the German trade would be permanently diverted to Yorkshire.

The Dodworth War Distress Committee met on the 20 November at the Mechanics' Institute to consider a resolution passed at the recent public meeting regarding the acceptance and maintaining of some Belgian refugees in the village. The outcome was satisfactory as it was disclosed that sufficient accommodation could be immediately provided at two locations to accommodate eleven persons.

A concert promoted by the members of the

Any further communication on this
subject should be addressed to—

The Secretary,
War Office,
London, S.W.

and the following number quoted.

100/Infantry/551.   (M.S.1.)

War Office,
London, S.W.

20th November, 1914.

Sir,

I am directed to inform you that you have been

appointed to command the Barnsley Battalion York and
Lancaster Regiment, with effect from the 17th of
September, 1914,

and I am to request that you will take up your duties as

soon as possible.

You will be granted the temporary rank of

Lieutenant Colonel in the Army.

The requisite notification as above will

appear in the London Gazette in due course.

I am,

Sir,

Your obedient Servant,

Col.

for Military Secretary.

Lieutenant Colonel J.Hewitt,
    Barnsley Battalion York and Lancaster Regt.
        B A R N S L E Y .

**Letter from War Office to Lieutenant-Colonel Joseph Hewitt, dated
20 November 1914.**

BELGIAN REFUGEES
IN BARNSLEY 1914

A group of Belgian refugees are photographed in Barnsley 1914. Old Barnsley

Darfield Ambulance Classes was held on Saturday, 21 November in the mixed schools, the proceeds being donated to the local Belgian Relief Fund, there being eight Belgian refugees residing in the village.

December 1914
The public of Barnsley and district were reminded that with Christmas only being a short time away, many worthy movements were in hand for providing local soldiers and sailors with suitable and acceptable gifts. Many had already been sent to the men at the front and to the sailors on the seas and it was hoped that the public would not forget the gallant men of their own district, who had at great sacrifice to themselves, left their homes, and in some cases their families to fight for their country.

In the prelude to the festive season the designs and patterns of beautiful dresses for the coming fashions by Madame Gwendolen Hope, were the talk among the ladies in the drawing rooms of many a home throughout Barnsley and district. Indeed, the stole and muff that were made up partly of fur and chiffon or partly of fur and velvet were creating a perfect furore in matters sartorial. It was said that the alliance was made for economy, certainly; for, although fur would be no dearer that winter than it had been for several seasons past, yet, owing to the enormous demand it had beforetime reached almost prohibitive figures. It was suggested that those possessors of small muffs and stoles, who had been eyeing them sadly and trying to wish them into growing bigger, may take heart of grace and bring them entirely up to date on the above suggestion. Ladies were further advised if your small treasured muff be sable, let the added part, whether it be chiffon or velvet, be of the exact sable shade; and the same remark applies to any other kind of fur. Black velvet and ermine is a very favourite combination this winter, and a black velvet muff edged with ermine, and perhaps with an ermine tail flung across, is a very enviable possession. For wear out of doors bright touches of colour are used on sombre-coloured costumes – on navy particularly, a little Eastern embroidery say adding great charm. If both costume and furs are dark a very cheerful touch may be added by a big bunch of artificial violets, or a bright coloured velvet rose nestling in the fur is a suitable object on which to gaze.

On the early evening of 2 December, at about half-past four, a terrible tramcar accident occurred in Barnsley, when a double-decker, travelling between Smithies and Barnsley, the property of the Barnsley and District Traction Company Limited, had got out of control and careered down the Eldon Street North incline. The car was driven by Harold Tingay of Worsbrough Common and the conductor was John Priestley, of Cope Street, Barnsley. Having arrived at the Eldon Street terminus, the driver having applied the brakes had occasion to leave the platform. During his temporary absence the car got into motion, attained gathering speed down the steep incline, and with tremendous momentum jumped the rails near the Prince of Wales's corner and crashed with terrific force into the general dealer's shop belonging to Mr J.C. Dodd. There were several passengers in the car when it set off on its perilous journey, but witnesses stated that the conductor, after trying unsuccessfully to apply the brakes, had jumped off the car near James Street, and that this desperate seeking of safety – the more dangerous because of the stone tramway track – was also attempted at the cost of minor injuries by another man and woman who leaped from the car. All the passengers were on the lower deck.

RUNAWAY TRAM AT BARNSLEY
7, INJURED
DECR 2ND 1914.

The runaway tram left the tracks at the bottom of Eldon Street and crashed into a shop belonging to Mr J.C. Dodd on Old Mill Lane. Old Barnsley

Those in the car were in a parlous plight, when it came to a halt after crashing into the dealer's shop, when extricated from their imprisonment, were all more or less suffering from broken limbs, cuts and bruises and shock. Help was quickly at hand, rendered by the Police Fire Brigade (who were all ambulance men), giving help to the injured, six of whom were removed as quickly as possible to the Beckett Hospital. One of the injured, 50-year-old widow, Mrs Sarah Hague, of Wakefield Road, Barnsley, later succumbed to her injuries and her death was followed a week later by that of 21

Beckett Hospital and Nurses Home, Barnsley.

Beckett Hospital where the injured from the tram crash were treated.

year-old Mrs Gladys Fitzgerald of 4 Maud's Terrace, Monk Bretton. At the subsequent inquest the jury found that death was accidentally caused, but there was carelessness on the part of the driver and the conductor.

Christmas in 1914, and Barnsley and district was unusually quiet. Current circumstances for the people of our Kingdom demanded that it should be, for the people of this great nation, this United Kingdom were under the subduing influence of opponents at sea or across the sea. In the town of Barnsley itself of music in the streets there appeared to be far less than usual; carol singers were scarce, and yet Christmas seemed to be spent by the majority in a manner which was becoming to all. The children, of course, enjoyed the tribute of gifts. In town and village the customary church services were held on Christmas Day, and in most instances the congregations were large. At the Beckett Hospital and the Union Workhouse there was no break in the traditions of the day and the usual bounty was distributed. The hospital population had increased considerably since the advent of war and wounded soldiers, whose comfort and enjoyment on this particular day was more than ever attended to.

Enquiry at the Post Office revealed the fact that whilst business had been great, there had been a marked falling off in the Christmas Eve postings. Many parcels for the soldiers at the front had been despatched from Barnsley and the immediate neighbourhood within the past fortnight, and the hope of everyone at home would have been that our brave lads had a real merry Christmas. A remarkably large number of soldiers had been seen about the streets during the holidays, the men in training being given leave to visit their families and friends. Many of the warriors entering into the true spirit of this most enjoyable of christian festivals, deservedly having earned what was no doubt a much appreciated break from the ordeals of military life, perhaps in some instance were a trifle too exuberant and

---

December 1914
21st
The first German air raid on England took place. An aeroplane dropped bombs in the sea near Dover.

24th
The second air raid on England took place when a German aeroplane dropped a bomb near Dover. The first bomb to be dropped on English soil.

25th
A British seaplane raid on Cuxhaven took place.

---

over indulgent, resulting in them exceeding their time-limit and had, of course, to go through the customary ordeal of being led back to the camp or barracks by court-martial. The influx was quite counter-balanced by the exodus. At the Barnsley railway stations there had been stirring scenes, but the traffic was got through all right, the officials being able to cope with the abnormal crowds. As to the weather, the all important factor at holiday times, on the whole, had been good. True, there was a lot of rain, but happily the greater part fell in the night-time and did not inconvenience the general public.

Every effort was made to ensure that the patients in the Beckett Hospital had a happy Christmastide, and to this end the acting matron (Sister Bevan) and the medical and nursing staff spared no effort. As usual, the wards were all appropriately decorated, a feature being a number of Belgian flags, artistically arranged, in honour of the Belgian wounded soldiers within the hospital. The patients in the hospital on Christmas Day numbered eighty-two, and included fifty-seven men, ten women and fifteen children. Of the men, sixteen were wounded soldiers from the fighting line, twelve being Belgians, and the remaining four British. On Christmas morning the nurses went through the various wards singing carols, and at 9.30 am the Blucher Street Choir paid their welcome annual visit, and did their utmost to make the day brighter for the patients.

Later, Father Christmas (in the 'genial person' of Dr Ewart Martin, house surgeon), presented each patient with a useful present. The usual Christmas dinner was served, the carvers being Messrs. H. Feasby, A. Whitham, J. Rouse, F.B. Bedford and Dr Martin. The festive spirit prevailed right through the day, and the patients spent as happy a Christmas as was possible under the circumstances. On Boxing Day the gifts from the Christmas tree were distributed by Mrs G.A. Bond, who was assisted by Mr R.F. Pawsey and an excellent evening concert was held, the artistes including Miss Hunt, Mr Richardson, Mr Howe and little Miss Ella Davidson, 'a promising elocutionist'. Miss Markwell was the accompanist. On Monday, 28th December the nurses had their annual dinner, and on Tuesday the maids had theirs.

The festive season at the Barnsley Union Workhouse was observed in the customary manner, the inmates having the usual treats and 'extras'. Everything possible was done to make the poor people happy and well provided for. Large quantities of holly and mistletoe decorated the wards and corridors, and the brightness of the scene was enhanced by Chinese lanterns. The Mayor of Barnsley, Councillor W.G. England JP visited

Barnsley Union Workhouse received its first inmates in 1852. It was built in Gawber Road and was closed in 1964 and demolished. The Barnsley District General Hospital was built on the site.

the Union Workhouse during the evening accompanied by the Board of Guardians. In addition to numerous gifts from outside friends and associations the male inmates received the customary Christmas extras of tobacco and the women gifts of fruit etc. The chairman of the Board of Guardians, Mr J.F.W. Peckett, gave a threepenny-piece to each child. A concert for the inmates was held in the dining room in the evening. On Christmas Day there were in the institution 144 men, 100 women, and 44 children, and all these needy people, thanks to the kind gifts and admirable arrangements, were able to pass the day in enjoyment and comfort.

At Lundwood Hospital the patients were splendidly entertained at Christmastide. Among the patients were fifteen wounded British soldiers and along with all the other patients all were sumptuously entertained. On Christmas Day turkey was the chief item on the menu, followed by plum puddings. The wards were beautifully decorated with evergreens. On Thursday, 31 December, the christmas tree was stripped and the many useful presents were distributed among the patients.

The annual distribution of toys to the children of the Ardsley Working Men's Club and Institute took place on Boxing Day in the Ardsley Oaks

Colonel Hewitt.

Recruits pose for a photograph holding their soup bowls outside one of their huts at Newhall camp.

Council Schools. Nine-hundred children assembled in the schools at 2 o'clock in the afternoon, and were supplied with toys, sweets and oranges.

Christmas Day at Newhall camp, Silkstone, was a memorable time for the men of the 1st Barnsley Battalion. Every effort had been made throughout the preceding week to ensure the troops would have a happy time and there being an abundance of good cheer. There was a tinge of frost in the air in the early morning but on the whole the weather was kind and the great festive day was a delightful one to all at the camp. For dinner, turkey, pheasant, roast beef, and plum pudding, with beer or minerals as desired, constituted the menu, and as there was an ample supply the 'big family' had every opportunity of satisfying the inner man to the full. Subsequently an entertainment was given in the Regimental Institute and the end of which Colonel Hewitt addressed the troops, and submitted amid much enthusiasm the toast: 'May we all meet again next Christmas Day.' At night, rabbit pies and mince pies were served, followed by a supply of cigarettes and tobacco.

On Boxing Day, the battalion at Newhall camp paraded for divine service at the Silkstone and Dodworth churches of various denominations. In the days that followed the troops actively pursued their training, including nightly operations which were successfully carried out.

Chapter Three

1915: War Takes A Grip

January 1915

The spirit of the festive season spilled over into the New Year and the residents of Barnsley and district partook of some of the enjoyable entertainments on offer. At the Pavilion, Duncan's Royal Scotch Collies topped the bill during the first week of the year, they being described as the 'acme of animal training', having appeared 'before their Majesties by Royal Command'. The excellent vaudeville production September Morn (presented by Messrs Edelsten and Burns) topped the bill at The Empire and was described as being surely one of the best and brightest of shows on the variety stage. Brimful of comedy, with an abundance of bright and catchy music, there wasn't a dull moment from opening to close. Mr Jack Rarty, the principal comedian, made a pronounced hit with his comic business and funny gags (all new by the way). Another of the great successes of the production was Miss Constance Garrett, a gifted young soprano, who decisively scored in the patriotic song 'The Land of the Red, Red Rose'.

**January 1915
1st**
HMS *Formidable* was sunk by a German submarine in the English Channel.

MEETINGS AND ENTERTAINMENTS

NEW EMPIRE PALACE,
BARNSLEY.

6-50 —Twice Nightly. —9-0

MONDAY, JANUARY 11th, 1915, and
Every Evening during the Week.

GRAND MATINEE PERFORMANCE
at 2 o'clock on SATURDAY, JAN. 16th.
Children—2s., 4d. and 6d.

MR. WALTER BISHOP PRESENTS HIS
GRAND NEW AND UP-TO-DATE
PANTOMIME, ENTITLED—

DICK WHITTINGTON
AND HIS CAT.

BARNSLEY'S FAVOURITE.

MISS EDNA LATONNE
As "DICK WHITTINGTON."

TIMES AND PRICES AS USUAL.
PRIVILEGE TICKETS SUSPENDED.

PRINCESS PICTURE PALACE.
TOWNEND, BARNSLEY.

7 & 9 | EVERY EVENING. | 7 & 9

MATINEES—Every Monday, and Saturday.
Commence at 3-30.

Week commencing Monday, Jan. 11th, 1915.

MONDAY, TUESDAY, WEDNESDAY,
NEW SENSATIONAL DRAMATIC
PICTURE.

The Mystery of D'Orcival

THE WESTERN PUGILIST.
A SPLENDID WESTERN DRAMA.

THURSDAY, FRIDAY, SATURDAY.
A VITAGRAPH MASTERPIECE.

SHADOWS OF THE PAST.
A Story of intense Human interest.

THE COURT OF DEATH
being the 13th Series in the
"ADVENTURES OF KATHLYN."

2d., 4d., 6d.

For six days, from Monday 4th at the Theatre Royal, Will H. Glaze's Company were to be seen in an entertainment described as the play of the year, *Mother Mine*, by Eva Elwes. Billed as an 'Enormous Attraction', Messrs Jason & Montgomery's Sensational problem play of intense heart-stirring interest *The Woman who DID Tell!* by Herbert Sidney was the main event at the New Empire Palace. The management were keen to point out that Barnsley favourite Miss Edna Latonne would be appearing the following week as the character Dick Whittington in the pantomime *Dick Whittington And His Cat*. The Princess Picture Palace at Townend, was showing on Monday, Tuesday and Wednesday *The Wrath of the Gods*, a most extraordinary and fascinating series, and a picture to leave a lasting impression, acted by the only Japanese leading lady. Audiences also assembled at the Globe Picture House, the star attraction being *In The Grip of Spies*, the picture being the third of the famous Sleuth Hound series.

On Thursday, 7 January, a concert in aid of the Belgian Relief Fund was held in the infant schoolroom at Silkstone, which raised a substantial sum. The members of the Silkstone Parish Church 'King's Messengers' presented an excellent children's play entitled *The Babes in the Wood*. The audience thoroughly enjoyed the quaint sayings, and sweet singing of the children, which demonstrated careful preparation and highly proficient training.

On the morning of Saturday, 9 January, 61-year-old Thomas Waring, who lived in lodgings at 22 Dove Row, Hoyle Mill, met with a strange accident which resulted in his death the following Wednesday. Mr Waring was a labourer in the employ of Messrs Horne Bros, of Abbey Farm, Monk Bretton. Whilst in charge of a two-wheeled cart, laden with manure and pulled by two horses (a shaft horse, lead by Mr Waring and a trace horse being attached to the cart) going up Dove Road, one of the wheels of the cart sank into a soft part of the road at an awkward corner, which had been excavated and refilled the previous day (in order that drainpipes could be repaired), causing the front horse to swerve.

Mr Waring was knocked down and a stone gatepost was also knocked over as the horse fell on him, causing severe injuries. Acute bronchitis which set in as a result of the injuries he had sustained, proved fatal, and Mr Waring died on the 13 January, during the afternoon. An inquest was held on Thursday, 14 January, before Mr P. P. Maitland, at the Old White Bear Inn, Hoyle Mill. Several witnesses who had seen the accident were called and gave a clear account of what had occurred.

The coroner said that whoever had the laying of the drainage pipes in hand ought to have made the road efficient for driving purposes, or temporarily fenced it off to keep people from driving over it, because it was that that had caused the accident. Had greater care been used in repairing the road, the accident might have been avoided. A verdict of 'accidental death' was recorded.

On the evening of Tuesday, 19 January a full parade of the Barnsley Home Defence Corps assembled at their headquarters, the West Riding Police Parade Hall, for the purpose of being inspected by Lieutenant Colonel J. Hewitt, who had been instructed by the War Office to report as to the organisation and efficiency of the Corps. Having satisfactorily seen both Company and Section go through the detail of their drill, Lieutenant Colonel Hewitt told the men he had much pleasure in complimenting them on their soldiery appearance, and the manner in which they had gone through their drill

The New Year Handicaps promoted by the officials of the Royston Midland Working Men's Club and Institute came to a conclusion on Sunday, 31 January, when about 200 members and invited friends were present. The prizes were presented by Mr G. Chapman.

February 1915

One of the Belgian refugees, named Cornelius Hermann, who came to live at Ardsley the week before Christmas, received funds from relations in Canada sufficient to pay the passage for himself and his wife. The couple are leaving on Saturday, 13 February, with the best wishes of the Ardsley people.

The Early Closing Order (under the Licensing Temporary Restrictions Act, 1914) recently put into operation by the West Riding Justices throughout the Staincross Division, was the subject of strong criticism

---

January 1915

19th
The first Zeppelin raid on Britain took place.

28th
The British Government make a definite decision to undertake a naval attack on the Dardanelles.

29th
Walney Island battery (Barrow-in-Furness) was shelled by a German submarine.

30th
The British Admiralty warned British merchant vessels to fly neutral or no ensigns in the vicinity of the British Isles.

February 1915
16th
The British Government decide to send a division to the Dardanelles.

18th
The German submarine blockade of Great Britain began.

19th
The Allied naval attack on the Dardanelles forts commenced.

at the monthly meeting of the Wombwell Urban District Council on Wednesday, 10 February. It was pointed out that whereas in Barnsley the public houses remained open until the usual hour – 11pm – and in the adjoining county police areas of Rotherham and Doncaster until 10pm, the houses in Wombwell and throughout the Staincross District were closed at 9pm. Protests came from all sections of the Council, and tradesmen asserted that their trade would be practically ruined if the permitted hours were mot extended.

The Clerk read out a resolution which he was instructed to forward to the justices of the Staincross Division. In the resolution stress was laid upon the disastrous effect which the Order will have on the general trade of the district. The resolution was carried unanimously.

In reply to a challenge by the ladies of the Hoyland Guild of Help for Soldiers and Sailors, the men organised a successful tea and concert on Friday, 19 February, Dr C.J. Montague Lawrence presided at the concert and the artistes were Mrs Gertrude Atkinson, Mr S. Green, Miss Mabelle Holt and Mr H. Holden. Miss Florence Hague and Mr P. J. Green were the accompanists.

A drowning fatality occurred in the Aire and Calder Canal, on the afternoon of Tuesday, 23 February, near the notorious '32-steps' (footway over the canal), between Barnsley and Mapplewell. A passer-by noticed a dead man floating in the water and he was afterwards identified as 68-year-old retired miner, John Thornton, who lived at Denton's Buildings, Blacker Lane, Mapplewell. During the inquest before Mr P.P. Maitland at Barnsley Town Hall, it transpired that Mr Thornton lived with his three sons, having retired six or seven years previously due to failing health. The deceased's son John, said his father had been a little depressed recently. On the day he died, he put his hat on at about 10.30 am and went out for his habitual walk. He said his father had been unwell lately and was complaining of headaches and had a bad cough but he had declined to see a doctor. Joseph Ledger, landlord of the Cricketers' Arms, Upper Carr Road, Mapplewell, said he had known John Thornton for twenty-five years. He said Mr Thornton came to his house shortly before one o'clock. He seemed all right apart from his cough; and seemed in good spirits and did not appear in any way depressed. Mr Thornton left the house about twenty minutes past three and during the whole time he was there only drank two pints of beer. When he left he was quite sober.

The '32-steps' footway over the Barnsley canal. John Thornton was found dead in the water about 50 yards from the steps. Old Barnsley

James W. Thorley, colliery stoker, of 61 James Street, Barnsley, said that about 4.30pm on Tuesday he spotted the deceased in the canal about 50 yards from the 32-steps. Having called out to him and receiving no response, he went to fetch a policeman. However, when Mr Thorley returned with Police Constable George Hayward of the Borough Police, the body had already been laid on the canal bank. The deceased was fully clothed apart from his hat. The coroner said there was a strong presumption of suicide in the case but it was not absolutely proved, as the deceased might have fallen into the water accidentally. His history was that he had had bad health for some time, and his son said he had got into a low sort of way. The verdict was: 'found drowned, having probably committed suicide whilst of unsound mind through illness'.

The point as to whether the Early Closing Order (recently enforced in the Staincross Division) affected clubs as well as public houses was raised at the Barnsley West Riding Court on Friday 19th, when John Gwynne, club secretary, of Royston, was charged on two summonses with selling intoxicating liquor at clubs during prohibited hours, he being secretary of both the Royston Midland Working Men's Club and the Royston Social

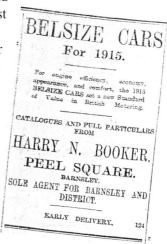

February 1915
24th
The first British Territorial Division (the North Midland) left England for France.

26th
'Liquid fire' was first used by the Germans on the Western Front.

Club. It was alleged by the prosecution and admitted by the defendant that the offences took place the previous Sunday, 14 February, when liquor was sold at both clubs between 12 noon and 12.30 pm. It was stated that the clubs' hours of opening on Sunday were 9.30 am–10.30 am, 12.30 pm–2 pm and 6 pm–10 pm. The proceedings were adjourned pending the results of a similar case in the High Court at Pontefract, which was awaiting a decision from the Home Secretary. Meanwhile, regarding the eventual outcome of the case in question, an undertaking was given that intoxicating drinks would not be sold at both clubs at Royston before 12.30 pm on Sundays.

On Saturday, 27 February, 39-year-old Sarah Ann McIntosh, who lived with her husband and family at 15 Charity Street, Monk Bretton, was the unsuspecting victim of a remarkable case of fatal alcohol poisoning. Late on Saturday Mrs McIntosh drank a pint of practically neat whisky very quickly and within a few minutes she had become unconscious. She died at about eleven o'clock on Sunday morning. The inquest was held at Monk Bretton before Mr P.P. Maitland on Monday morning. The jury found that the deceased died from heart failure due to acute alcohol poisoning. Thomas McIntosh, the deceased woman's husband said they had only been living in Monk Bretton for three weeks. His wife had been a healthy woman but had been drinking heavily for the last seven years. She had 'drunk' most of his wages for he had given her plenty of money. She drank both beer and spirits but lately she had seemed a little better in that respect. On Saturday night he went out to go to the Cudworth Picture Palace, leaving his wife, his youngest daughter and his 14-year-old son, Clifford in the house (Clifford was promptly sent out to the Star where his mother told him he was to get a pint bottle of Scotch whisky). Mr McIntosh returned about ten o'clock and found his wife laid on the hearthrug fully dressed. She was unconscious and appeared to be drunk. She had been in a similar condition many times before, and the family let her lie where she was in order that she could sleep it off.

Dr Edmund Walsh said he was called to Charity Street early in the afternoon and arrived at about one o'clock. The deceased, who was sitting on a chair was already dead, and had probably been so for a couple of hours. Dr Walsh made a post-mortem examination. The deceased was well nourished and there were no external marks of any injury. The brain was congested and the stomach was dilated and very much congested. There was also a smell of alcohol. The doctor added that the alcohol poisoning was acute and would be accounted for if the deceased had drunk a large quantity of whisky neat. She had probably been drinking for some time and a large dose at the end had finished her.

The coroner described the case as a very shocking one. The dead woman had given way to excessive drinking for some little time, but nothing approaching this. Why she drank a pint of whisky at the finish he did not know, but directly the husband turned his back and went out to the picture palace she evidently thought she would have a good drink, as she would call it, and sent the lad for the whisky. She finished it off in a very few minutes with the result that she was now dead. It was not really a case of suicide but it was a suicidal act. The jury found that the deceased died of heart failure due to acute alcohol poisoning.

March 1915

Soon after nine o'clock on Tuesday evening, 2 March, many of the inhabitants of Darfield were severely alarmed by an earthquake shock which lasted about five seconds. Several complained of houses being severely shaken, the shock in some places being so great as to dislodge various articles of furniture. Many people felt a distinct bump and fears were entertained that an explosion must have occurred in one of the neighbouring collieries. Fortunately, such fears were groundless. Others thought that the Zeppelins had at last arrived and began to take precautions against a possible attack. The shock was also distinctly felt at Little Houghton. The cause of the earthquake was believed to have been rooted in subsidence within underground workings.

Earlier the same evening an earthquake had alarmed the residents of Darfield, at a pleasing ceremony in the Wath-upon-Dearne Urban District Council meeting. Dennis, Turnbull, 13-year-old son of William Turnbull, tailors' cutter, of Townend, was made the recipient of a vellum certificate of the Royal Humane Society for gallantry in saving a drowning child of 3 from the canal at Wath on 10 September last. Mr W. Riley, the chairman, said that he was generally proud of the courageous boy, and it was a source of considerable satisfaction to the Council to know that he learned his swimming in Wath. Councillor Hallatt said that if the sole fruit of their bath scheme was the saving of one precious life, and

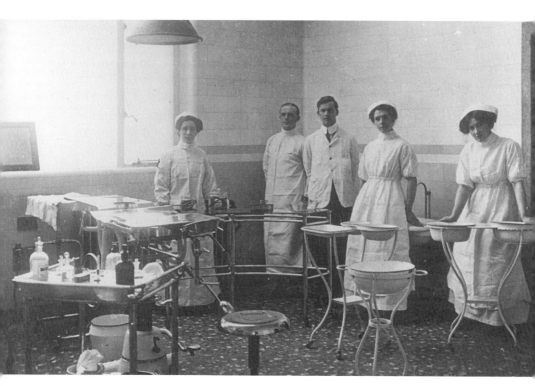

Medical staff at the Beckett Hospital, Barnsley, where William Harris, aged 8, was taken following his accident in Wombwell.

the opportunity to bring out the heroism of a Wath youth, they were handsomely compensated and justified.

On the afternoon of Saturday, 13 March, the thoughtless action of an excited Wombwell crowd waiting for a motor-bus resulted in the death of an 8-year-old boy. William Harris was waiting with his father and little sister at the top of Church Street for the bus to take them to Barnsley. A big crowd was waiting behind them. At three o'clock a charabanc drew up and the crowd immediately rushed for it. Little William Harris, his father and several others at the front of the queue were pushed over and the boy was dragged under the vehicle. His right leg was terribly crushed, and the doctors at the Beckett Hospital, to where he was swiftly taken, decided that amputation was necessary. The shock of his injuries was too great for the little boy to endure and he died on Monday morning.

The members of the Stainborough, Dodworth and District Rifle Club held a meeting at the Pheasant Inn, Dodworth, presided over by Mr

John Archer. Captain W. J. Fisher, secretary, said the range had been kept open all the winter and had done good work owing to the fact that a large number of men connected with the Barnsley battalions had practised shooting there. It was decided the club's season should be opened on Easter Saturday when a couple of prizes should be competed for.

**March 1915
18th**
The Allied naval attacks on the Dardanelles was repulsed. The French battleship *Bouvet* and British battleships *Irresistible* and *Ocean* were sunk.

The Barnsley Male Voice Choir, formed less than two years ago, gave their first open concert on the night of Sunday, 21 March, in the Empire Palace, Barnsley. The effort was in aid of the Barnsley Patriotic Fund and was a distinct success from both a musical and financial standpoint. An appreciative crowd filled every part of the Empire, and the concert passed off in a way which reflected the greatest credit on the officials. The lengthy programme was gone through without a hitch and it was noted that all the items had been chosen with considerable taste. The singing of the choir showed clear signs of careful and thorough training, demonstrated by the skills of the conductor Mr Charles Thompson.

A parents' evening was held in connection with the Grimethorpe Infants School on Friday, 26 March, when the children went through a short programme consisting of songs, dances and games. The evening's proceedings opened with a 'Grand March' when the children dressed in fancy attire marched round the hall to suitable national airs. It was generally agreed that the effect was very pretty indeed. There was a large audience and the sum of £9 10s. was raised which was sent to the Comforts for the Soldiers' Fund.

Sir Joseph Walt, Bart, MP, paid a visit to Barnsley on Monday, 29 March, and remained in the borough overnight. Attired in khaki, by virtue of the position he held as Deputy-Lieutenant, the member for the Division, first saw the men of the 14th Service Barnsley Battalion in the town, and then proceeded to Noblethorpe Hall, to inspect the troops of the 13th Service Barnsley Battalion, who paraded in Noblethorpe Park. In the evening Sir Joseph went to the 'first house' at Barnsley Empire, where he made an appeal for recruits. He was accompanied by Acting Colonel Raley. In addressing the audience he said he had paid many visits to the Barnsley Division in the last twenty years, but never before had he come before them in the king's uniform. It might be news to them to know that he had the king's commission for more than twenty years, but as he was too old to go into the fighting line, having therefore not worn his uniform recently. But the king had given instructions that all his deputy lieutenants on occasions as such he was attending and during the present crisis, wear the service uniform. Whilst referring to his experience amongst the wounded in France recently, where he had seen an ambulance train come in, most of the wounded were suffering because their feet had gone wrong, having spent too long spells at a time in the trenches. He said he was attending the theatre that night to appeal to the young men of Barnsley to come forward and join Colonel Raley's battalion in order to go and help the other chaps at the front, so that they could have only a reasonably short spell in the trenches, and then out again. Sir Joseph said the men at Newhall Camp, who he had since and inspected in Noblethorpe Park earlier that day, were the most soldiery like lot he had seen yet, a comment which was met with loud cheers. Continuing, Sir Joseph said Colonel Raley needed 350 more men to complete the Second Barnsley Battalion, and he was there to ask you men to consider whether it was not their duty in this supreme crisis to come forward and offer their services. He specially applied to young men who had no family responsibilities. The young men so far had not shown the same degree of patriotism that many of the married men of Barnsley had done by coming forward so magnificently, and the large proportion who had enlisted so far were married men with family

responsibilities. Sir Joseph concluded by saying, 'I am sure I shall have from a patriotic Barnsley audience a very practical response.'

April 1915

Concerns had been raised in recent months that considerable pilfering had taken place from shop fronts in Barnsley, some answers to which were explained at Barnsley courthouse on Thursday, 8 April, when six children (five girls and a boy), all under fourteen, were charged with numerous thefts, while the mother of two of the children, Harriet West, married, of Graham's Orchard, Barnsley, was charged as acting as receiver of the stolen property.

It was clear from the evidence concerned that the children had formed themselves into a gang, their one objective being systematic thieving. All the children pleaded guilty. Harriet West, who had been in custody for nearly three weeks was charged with receiving the stolen articles, which amounted to a considerable quantity, knowing them to have been stolen. She admitted that she had received the articles, but said she had no idea they had been stolen.

Addressing the children, the mayor (Councillor England) said it

13th Battalion en masse in Noblethorpe Park, Silkstone.

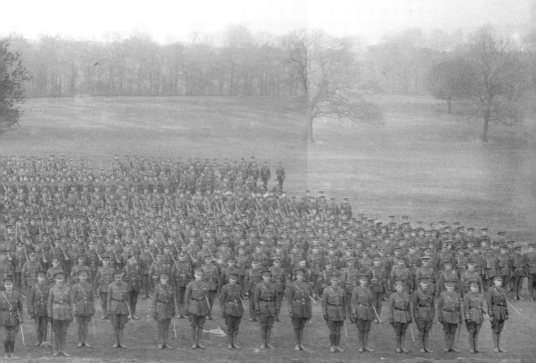

was a terrible thing for little girls to go about doing such things. All of them, with the exception of 12-year-old Mabel Phillips (who had made admissions deemed to be more serious than those of the other children), would be put on probation, and their parents would have to pay the costs and look after them better in the future. As for Mabel Phillips, she was committed to a reformatory until she was seventeen. Mrs West, who must have known very well that the articles were stolen, was fined 30s. with the option of 21 days' imprisonment.

The government's recent hint that it may be found necessary to resort to the total prohibition of the sale of alcoholic liquors have had no effect on the trade generally. There was, so far, an entire absence of 'panic orders', and enquiries made by the press in London's West End among many leading wine and spirits merchants showed that their orders were on the normal level, and in only one case was an increase reported.

Mail bags packed with letters concerning the drink evil were arriving at Downing Street addressed to Mr Lloyd George. A large staff, specially engaged for the work of classification, sorted through the letters which numbered between 30,000–40,000.

Mr Will Thorne, MP, commented, 'I think it would be a huge mistake to close down all public houses, because, in my opinion, it would defeat the objects the government have in view. If the government were to deal with the men in the same way as they are dealing with the women, namely not to sell any drink to them before eleven o'clock in the morning, I think this would have the desired effect.'

A mass meeting of smelters, furnacemen and armour-plate workers on government contracts was held in Sheffield, at which a resolution was passed pointing out that their work necessitated a demand for drink after discharging and recharging furnaces. To close public houses would cause great resentment and perhaps a general strike.

At the Barnsley West Riding Court on Wednesday, 14 April, Arthur Smith, licensee of the Gate Inn, Dodworth, was summoned for supplying beer to soldiers during prohibited hours. Mr E. J. Rideal appeared for the defendant, and said his client pleaded guilty.

Superintendent McDonald said that on 15 February an order was served upon the West Riding police by Colonel Howe, of Pontefract, who was the competent military authority in the district of the Defence of the Realm Act. Copies of that order were given to the various innkeepers, and one of its conditions was that members of HM forces should not be supplied with drink, except between the hours of 12 and 1 mid-day and 6–9 at night.

At 9.25 am on 7 April, Sergeant Smith visited the Gate Inn, and there found four soldiers drinking beer. The sergeant drew the landlord's attention to the men's presence and received the reply that he thought the men were all right as they were on a pass. When Sergeant Smith told Mr Smith that he would be reported, he received the reply, 'Well, they can get it in Barnsley while they are on a pass, so I thought I might as well serve them as for them to get it there.' All witness evidence having been given, Mr Rideal addressing the bench said, 'There is no doubt, your worships, that a technical offence has been committed.'

The chairman, Mr T. Norton, addressing the defendant, said, 'This is a very grave offence, serving recruits in this way. You must have read in the papers and known from the talk about it what very serious consequences follow when soldiers are allowed to obtain drink in this way. Instead of fitting themselves for the object for which they have enlisted, they become incapacitated from duty. The penalty for this offence is £50, but as this is the first case of its kind brought before this court, in your case we will reduce it to £10. I may tell you that if any further cases of this character come before this court, we shall inflict the full penalty of £50, and if fining people will not do it, other means will have to be tried.'

On 17 April, the *Barnsley Chronicle* reported:

'Careful enquiries among the leaders of the coalminers of Great Britain reveal a general feeling of opposition to the proposal for the prohibition of alcohol during the period of the war. It is admitted that there is a good deal of irregular working on the part of the coalminers but it is asserted that the loss of working time from the drinking habits of the men is inconsiderable. The enlistment of something like 150,000 men has removed this surplus from the pits, so the coal output at the moment of national stress is reduced.'

On Saturday, 17 April, the Stainborough and Dodworth Rifle Club opened their season, when there was a large attendance of members and

Second Battle of Ypres. Men of the 1/5 York and Lancaster Regiment, soon after their arrival at the northen end of the Ypres Salient.

Gallipoli landings. A view looking towards V Beach which is in the process of being transformed into a supply depot.

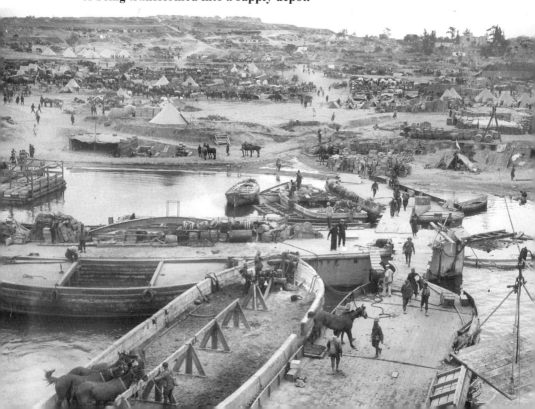

April 1915
22nd
Battles of Ypres began – also known as the Second Battle of Ypres.

25th
Allied troops land in Gallipoli.

recruits. The talk amongst members was a recently mooted proposal for the formation of a ladies' branch, which some members expressed the opinion that such a branch would undoubtedly be a great success under the able training of such noted 'shots' as Mrs Mackenzie and Miss Symonds, who had that day demonstrated their expertise.

On Friday, 30 April, Mr Lloyd George introduced a further Bill to amend the Defence of the Realm Act, when he announced to the House the steps the government proposed to take for dealing with the alleged excessive drinking by workmen in the war munitions areas. He quoted many facts as to the loss of time and slackness in the shipyards, armaments works and among transport workers, which he said was very largely caused by excessive drinking. To deal with the problems he proposed to double the duty on whisky, to impose a graduated surtax on beer according to its specific gravity, and to quadruple the duty on wine. He outlined as far as he could the effect of these proposals on the revenue.

The government also proposed to take complete control of the sale of drink in war areas during the period of the war, and compensation would be given for the sequestration of all interests, whether public houses or other properties.

May 1915

By the beginning of May measles were very prevalent in Hemingfield and there were many absences from school. The recent high scoring at the monthly completion at Hemingfield Rifle Club for the silver spoon, was the talk of the village. Shot at three distances – 25 yards, 50 yards and 100 yards, with a maximum of 100 points for each distance, the secretary, Mr W. Huddlestone, was the winner with a score of 277, Mr W. Beaumont was second with 235 points and Mr J. Watkin, third, with 220 points.

On the night of Wednesday, 5 May, an army order was published which provided that:

'during the remaining period of the present war the age of enlistment or re-enlistment, in the Territorial Force will be from 19 to 38, instead of from 17 to 35 years, as hitherto, except in cases of Inns of Court, Officers'

PRICE ONE PENNY

13th SERVICE
Barnsley Battalion
YORK AND LANCS. REGT.
(1st Barnsley Battalion)

50 RECRUITS STILL WANTED.

The opportunity to join this Batt. has been seized by a good number.

Just a Chance left to Join your Pals.

Enlist at Once—You must not Delay.

APPLY TO

Officer-Commanding Newhall Camp, near Barnsley; or at the Battalion Barnsley Office, 1, "Chronicle" Buildings, Pitt Street.

Training Corps and Artists' Rifles. Ex-non-commissioned officers, Regulars and Territorials, not below the rank of sergeant, may be re-enlisted up to the age of 50; other ex-non-commissioned officers of the Territorial Force up to 45. Enlistments for general hospitals will be restricted to men between 17 and 19, and over 38. Shoeing smiths, saddlers and telegraphists may be enlisted up to the age of 50... No ex-officer under the age of 40 will be accepted unless medically unfit for more active duties, and in no case will officers over 60 be taken for this service... Establishment will be for service in any place in the United Kingdom. No man under the age of 38, medically fit to perform the ordinary duties of a soldier, will be enlisted in these companies, and no man over 50 will be accepted.'

Major Logan Ellis, who recently inspected the Barnsley Defence Corps, sent the following letter to the corps, which was reproduced in the *Barnsley Chronicle* on 8 May:

To the Commandant and Members.... Since last I had the pleasure of inspecting you I can see a considerable improvement in your drill and bearing, and from what I hear you have made strides in rifle shooting. A good local knowledge of the country round about, say for 10 miles, is now what you want to acquire, a knowledge of scouting, etc. I come in contact with recruiting in all its branches. I have to be up in who to accept and who not to accept amongst men equally eligible for the infantry. Why? Because the man who is a skilled worker and can

May 1915
7th

The RMS *Lusitania* was sunk by the German submarine 'U-20' off Queenstown in the North Atlantic Ocean, near Old Head of Kinsale, Ireland. Of the 1,959 passengers and crew aboard there were only 761 survivors. [This turned international opinion strongly against Germany.]

make shells or parts of shells, guns, or parts of guns, is not in his right place if he goes to the trenches. He can do more for his King and country by utilising his trade. There are others who although not actually making shells or guns are helping in other ways, they too, with the approval of your committee and myself is of eligible age for the Army are doing their best work where they are. And not only this but, all those I have mentioned can in addition join the volunteer forces and in a sense can feel that they are doing you double duty. To get every man to work where his best skill is utilised is going to be our best way through this great crisis, and it is for the permanent good of our country that every man should work shoulder to shoulder and feel it is his proud privilege to put forth his utmost energies against our common foe in whatever he is called upon to do. Continue the good work you are doing. Be in your right place (your own conscience will tell you where that place is). Work with all your Yorkshire might and then when we have won the day you will feel that you have acquitted yourselves like men and you will be proud of having kept up your reputation as Englishmen. The only people I am sorry for in this great struggle are those who may be wavering and are not putting forth their full energies in this great cause of Right against everything that is wrong. Continue your best energies to get recruits for the Army, not only by your good example as volunteers, but by utilising your every day opportunities of pointing out to those young men you know who ought to enlist in the Army, the necessity of their doing so at once...'

The afternoon of Wednesday, 12 May, was a memorable one at Newhall camp. Lieutenant-Colonel Hewitt gave a farewell luncheon in the Regimental Institute to which were invited the officers of both the First and Second Barnsley battalions, and a number of lady and gentlemen friends, including members of the Barnsley Corporation. The capacious building had been appropriately decorated for the occasion, and the scene that presented itself to the visitor was truly British.

Little work was done of an ordinary character in Barnsley on Thursday, 13 May. Thousands of locals from all over Barnsley and District left their labours and turned out to take a last look at the battalions which were born in the town, and to bid them farewell and God-speed. As early as 9.30 am people began to congregate around Market Hill and as the morning advanced the crowd rapidly grew. A big proportion of the men of the battalions being drawn from the surrounding districts

The short-cut bridge to Newhall Camp.

contributed their share of the enormous crowds that were flocking into the centre of Barnsley. The greatest crush was in the vicinity of Market Hill and Court House Station. Flags and bunting were in evidence in all the principal streets.

The Second Battalion was the first to depart. They paraded on Market Hill at 11.30 am, and at the same time the Mayor of Barnsley (Councillor W.G. England, JP), and members and officials of the Corporation assembled in the Town Hall, afterwards walking to where the troops gathered on Market Hill. The mayor was in his uniform as Hon. Colonel of the 1st Battalion, and he also wore his robes and insignia of office. The mayor and Corporation faced the men in front of the Corn Exchange, and brief but feeling messages of farewell were delivered. After the singing of the National Anthem, the mayor and other gentlemen representing the civic life of the town bade the troops farewell. Acting Colonel Raley thanked them on behalf of the officers, non-commissioned officers and men, thanked them from the bottom of his heart for the send-off. The speeches having being concluded, hearty cheers were given for the mayor, mayoress and Colonel Raley, before the troops left the Hill, the crowd sang 'Auld Lang Syne'.

The march then began to the railway station, Cooper's Royal Brass and Reed Band leading. The mayor and other members of the Corporation followed, and then came the battalion marching with full kit, and with soldiery bearing. On route many women were in tears and frequent last kisses were snatched by mothers, wives and sweethearts. The station was closed to the general public for the time being but there were great scenes of enthusiasm on the platform. The departure was scheduled for 12.30 pm, and the men passed the time in singing popular songs, the band striking up 'Tipperary', to the delight of the boys in khaki. As the troops entrained those on the platform joined heartily in singing 'Auld Lang Syne', finishing with the National Anthem as the train left

Officers and Men of the 13th Battalion at Barnsley Court House Station, en route to Rugeley, Cannock Chase. The mayor, Lieutenant-Colonel England, wearing his military uniform beneath his scarlet chief magistrates robes and insignia of mayoral office, is standing next to Lieutenant-Colonel Hewitt, waiting to see them off.

May 1915
23rd
The Italian Government order mobilisation and declare war against Austria and Germany .

25th
HMS *Triumph* was sunk by a submarine off the Dardanelles.

the station. 'A' and 'B' companies left first, the remainder travelling by the 2.10 pm train, when similar scenes were witnessed.

Whitsuntide in Barnsley and District was favoured by perfectly ideal weather, and had not the country been in such a turmoil consequent upon the European War, the festivities would have ranked as the most successful on record. All excursion traffic having been stopped, the trips usually indulged in by scholars and teachers at the various Sunday schools were abandoned, and the customary festivities were enjoyed in the immediate vicinity of the schools. A few parties were made up for motor spins, but short journeys were the general order. Barnsley wore a distinctly holiday appearance on Whit Monday and Tuesday, all the leading shops being closed, but at most of the collieries throughout the entire area, there was only one 'play day'. On the market ground the customary feast paraphernalia was in evidence, though said to be in a more diluted form than in years gone by.

The appointment of Admiral Sir Henry Broadwardine Jackson to be First Sea Lord of the Admiralty aroused great interest and considerable satisfaction in Barnsley and district of which he was a native. Sir Henry, now 60 years of age, was born at Darfield Rectory, where for ten years the Jackson family resided, at a time it was not being used by the then Rector of Darfield. Sir Henry is a son of the late Mr Henry Jackson, linen manufacturer and bleacher, of Barnsley and Cudworth. The Jacksons are a very old Barnsley family, having been connected with the town for generations.

Soldiers from Silkstone Camp taking a short break during exercises in bridge building in Cannon Hall park.

June 1915

At the beginning of the month, Hoyland Common newsagent Mr George Crookson received the following letter from Private William Crookson of the Yorkshire and Lancaster Regiment:

'...I am keeping well at present, but I cannot say for how long, for we are under fire here, so you can bet we are not so happy, at least not so happy as we should like to be. We came out of the trenches last Sunday night, May 16th, after a very hard time. We had a hot time, I can tell you, for our big guns started blowing things up, and German trenches were being blown into the air. It's a bit hard lines for the Germans to be killed like that, but it has to be dome, or the war will never be over. We had sent about a dozen shells over when the German guns had a go, and a shell dropped into D Company's trench, killing two of our men and wounding two others. But at the right of us our big guns have been firing for six or seven days, and the Germans must have lost men, and we as well, for that matter. After coming out of the trenches on Sunday night our platoon had to stop at a little farm just behind the trenches in case a working party should be wanted to dig trenches or carry wire or anything else to the firing line. I would like to say when the war will be over, but I cannot see the end yet. We shall want a lot more men yet, so the young chaps at Hoyland Common will have to come and do their bit, and then they will know something. Before I came out the papers said the Germans could not shoot, but for myself, I think they are better shots than we are, for if you put your head up in the trenches for half a minute you are a dead man. It is not so bad here in our trench, but it's bad going in and out, for we get all the cross fire from the other trenches. I think it's time our M.P.'s let us fight like the Germans are doing, for we are getting sick of having our hands nailed down and not being able to fight with the same things as they are

---

June 1915
2nd
A blockade of the coast of Asia Minor was announced by the British Government.

Increased Separation Allowances

for soldiers' wives and children.

FROM MARCH 1st the Separation Allowances paid by the Government to the wives and children of the soldiers have been increased, so that the total weekly payment to the family, if the soldier makes the usual allotment from his pay, is now as follows:—

	Corporal or Private.	Sergeant.
Wife per week	12/6	15/-
Wife and 1 child per week	17/6	20/-
Wife and 2 children, per week	21/-	23/6
Wife and 3 children, per week	23/-	25/6
and so on with an addition of 2/- for each additional child		
Each Motherless child	5/-	

To wives living at the time of enlistment in the London area, a further sum of 3/6 per week is paid as long as they continue to live there.

From February 1st, 1915, Separation Allowance is payable for all children up to the age of 16 years. This includes adopted children.

Allowances for other Dependants.

If an unmarried soldier has supported a dependant for a reasonable period, and wishes the support he gave to be continued, the Government will help, during the war, by making a grant of Separation Allowance, provided he will contribute part of his pay.

Full particulars can be obtained at any Post Office.

God Save the King.

using. If we started fighting, like the Germans are doing it would not be a long job, and not till we do will there be an end to it...'

During the first week of the month, until Wednesday, *The Scarlet Band* attracted fairly large audiences at the Theatre Royal, which was followed on Friday and Saturday by Ouida's ever popular play *Moths*, in which Mr Herbert Pearson took the role of Prince Sergius Zouroff, and Miss Maisie Hanbury that of Vere Herbert. At the Empire, a rattling good all-round programme was provided. Topping the bill was the Great Wieland, the famous dextrous humorist, guaranteed never to fail to create laughter. Frank Hartley, the all British juggler, topped the bill at the Pavilion, supported by a programme that could only be described as 'excellent'.

Ideal weather favoured the 29th annual Dodworth Musical Festival, held on Sunday, 6 June, in aid of the Beckett Hospital, the proceedings taking place in a field at the rear of the Thornley Arms, kindly lent by Councillor A. Dyson. Events took place in the afternoon and evening and raised the impressive sum of £25 12s. 10½d.

A tragic affair occurred in the evening of Saturday, 12 June, in the Prince of Wales Hotel, Eldon Street North, Barnsley. The landlord, 58-year-old Arthur Guest, had occasion to forcibly eject a customer, Michael Brumigham, miner, of 39 Old Mill Lane, who had been requested to leave, because he had had too much to drink. The highly intoxicated Brumigham returned twice and Mr Guest and his son, Arthur, had to forcibly turn him out of the premises each time. Immediately afterwards, Arthur Guest returned inside and went into the kitchen, where shortly he collapsed and died. At the inquest held before Mr P.P. Maitland on Monday, 14 June, at the Town Hall, having heard evidence from several witnesses, Dr Horoyde said that when he saw the deceased on Saturday he had just died. He said he was of the opinion that death was due to syncope from a fatty heart accelerated by excitement. The coroner said the evidence showed that the deceased man was able to conduct his business but now and again he showed signs of breathlessness, and evidently he had what is known as a fatty heart, and it was in that condition that any sudden excitement or anything like a struggle would be very dangerous for him. The evidence was to the effect that the man Brumigham did not actually assault the inn-keeper, but was simply trying to resist being put out. He may have pushed a bit but not after the nature of an assault.

At this point in the proceedings, Michael Brumigham, who was present but had not been called as a witness, asked to be allowed to make a statement, and the coroner permitted him to do so. He said he had never said a wrong word to the deceased and never laid hands on him. He did not remember refusing to go out of the public house. The affair had hurt him as much as it had hurt the relatives. He thought a lot about the gentleman, who was a friend of his.

The jury returned the following verdict: '… died from syncope due to heart disease accelerated by excitement in putting Brumigham, who was the worse for drink, out of his house.'

The coroner turned to Brumigham and addressing him, said:

'You were there all that time till your mind really became a blank, and you cannot now remember what took place. It is evident from that that you had such a quantity of beer that you were certainly in such a state that you ought to be turned out, and you were turned out. You didn't like going out and you resisted to a certain extent. You came back and you had again to be put out. If the evidence had shown that you not only resisted being put out, but that you used actual violence, you would be in a most serious position. You be careful in the future or else you will be getting into a very serious condition.'

A short, but brisk recruiting effort, was made at Houghton on Saturday, 12 June, amongst the colliers at Houghton Main. Sergeant Bambridge who, as an old Midland League footballer, was well-known in Barnsley sporting circles, and Corporal Morris, addressed two pit-gate meetings. Their appeals were brief, but were sharp and to the point. Both were listened to with enhanced interest by the fact that they had both come over from the fighting line in France, and Sergeant Bambridge, who had been awarded with the coveted Distinguished Service Medal, wore this honour.

A case of much interest to 'clubmen' was heard at the Barnsley West Riding Court on Friday, 18 June, when John Gwynne, secretary of the Midland Working Men's Club, Royston and the Royston Social Club, was summoned for selling intoxicating liquor during prohibited hours. The defendant was summoned in respect of each club; the defendant was before the Brewster Sessions in February on the same charges but the case was adjourned pending a High Court decision on a similar case at Pontefract, which had been remitted to the Court of Appeal.

Mr Rideal, who appeared for the defendant, said his client pleaded guilty. Mr Farmer, from the office of the county solicitor prosecuted. Having outlined the events of the case heard in February, Mr Farmer continued that it appeared that the club authorities were advised that this part of the Order, regarding permitted hours, did not apply to them, this notwithstanding that the Order was quite clear in its terms, and that copies of it had been served upon the defendant who, however, chose to disregard it.

Referring to the outcome of the Pontefract case, Mr Farmer said, 'This practice must stop and it is to be hoped that the publicity to be given to those proceedings today, will bring home to those club people that this Order exists and that it has got to be obeyed...' Mr Farmer pointed out that Mr Justice Avory said in his judgement, 'It is the duty of the court to give practical effect to legislation, and not give effect to mere casuistry. The plain meaning of that, added Mr Farmer, is that the clubs must not remain open for the consumption of liquor from 9pm until the hour next day when public houses may open. I believe at the last hearing that the defendant gave an undertaking that they would not do so and they have kept the undertaking.'

The Chairman of the Bench, Mr C. Howard Taylor, concluded, saying, 'There will be a fine of £2 costs in each case.'

The first of a series of plays to be given at the Theatre Royal during the succeeding weeks was the ever popular drama *The King's Romance*. Mr E. Vivian Evans, whose company it is, is well-known amongst patrons of the Barnsley Theatre and, as on the occasion of his former visits, large audiences have assembled. *The King's Romance*, is, as the title indicates, a romantic play of the highest order, and certainly one of Mr Edmond's best efforts. He appears in the role of Prince Andreas and is backed by a powerful array of artistes. The star attraction at the Empire during the same week was the burlesque *Who'll Have It?* presented by a first-class London company, including Mr Alf Daniels and Miss Anna Moon. Following this will be London's latest musical offering *Glad to See You*. At the Pavilion, paying a welcome return, Vivana and Company topped the bill, presenting a delightful sketch entitled 'The Toy Shop' and the cast included Mark Lupino, a comedian 'racy of the soil'.

Mr W. Allen JP, chairman of Hoyland

Barnsley Pals drilling in bayonet fighting at Silkstone Camp.

Nether Urban District Council informed the members at their monthly meeting on Monday, 28 June, that it was his intention to call a public gathering on the Market Place, with a view to furthering the Home Defence Corps Movement. Mr Allen explained that at Hoyland Common a branch of the Corps had already been formed and the desire expressed that a section should be formed at Elsecar and Hoyland, to be ultimately attached to either the Barnsley or the Hoyland Common Branch. Mr Allen said he hoped it would not be necessary for the old men of this country to have to go into the trenches, but that even was quite possible. When they considered that around the British Isles there were one thousand miles of trenches dug for their defence and occupied by Regulars of the Army, it was quite on the cards that if these men were drawn upon to go into the fighting line their places would have to be taken by those already at home. The chairman concluded by saying, 'I was at a meeting of the Barnsley Home Defence Corps at Barnsley last Friday night and it is hoped to get a strong branch there. I may say that it is the intention of the Barnsley members to come round the districts to gather in all they can, and in view of that we here in Hoyland think we should move in the matter and that it would be far better for us to have our own Corps,' to which there was a resounding, 'Hear, hear.'

July 1915

The annual report of Barnsley Football Club was issued by the committee at the beginning of the month. It read:

'In submitting the report and accounts for the year ending April 30th 1915, your Directors regret having to record a loss of £2,399 10s, 2d. on the year's working, compared with a profit last year of £938 10s. 1d. This is chiefly brought about on account of a reduction in receipts for player's transfers of £2,105; in gate receipts of £1,637 16s. 1d.; and in season ticket receipts of £226. 10s 3d.

The two last named are losses due to the war, and also with regard to the gates, to the bad weather conditions. In nearly all the items of expenditure as substantial saving has been effected, £210 spent in travelling, training and hotel expenses, and £179 on ground maintenance.

The deplorable financial result is the more to be regretted, inasmuch, as the success of the team in the Second League engagements was the greatest in the history of the club. The Directors regret that the whole-hearted efforts of the players to gain promotion just failed to achieve success. As the third position in the League was obtained, and only one match lost on our own ground, it is only fair to assume that, under normal conditions, the gate receipts would have been quite 50 per cent larger. The

13th & 14th **SERVICE**

Barnsley Battalions

YORK AND LANCS. REGTS.

6th Company to be Raised.

There is still an opportunity to Join your Pals.

The War Office have authorised the raising of the 6th Company.

ENLIST THIS DAY!

APPLY TO

Newhall Camp, near Barnsley; at the Battalion Barnsley Office, 1, "Chronicle" Buildings, Pitt Street, or at the Public Hall.

God Save the King.

average first team gate was £122; and that for the Central League matches was £17 17s. The League: 38 played, 22 won, 13 lost, 3 drawn, 47 points; Central League: 38 played, 13 won, 18 lost, 7 drawn, 33 points.

We have pleasure in recording the fact that the Reserve team won the Sheffield Challenge Cup. Your Directors have reluctantly decided to withdraw from the Central League and have been admitted members of the Midland League. We think it proper to record the fact that every facility and encouragement was given to the players to join the National Forces, and we are pleased to say that four players have enlisted. Practically the whole of the remainder of the players are now engaged in the work of providing munitions for the war.'

In 3 July edition of the *Barnsley Chronicle* an article appeared on page eight placed in among the district news with the heading: MUNITIONS WORK BUREAUX: 'In connection with the above scheme for Volunteers for the makings of munitions of War, Bureaux are now open at the following addresses in this district: The Town Hall, Barnsley; The Town Hall, Penistone: 30, Barnsley Road, Wombwell.'

A well-organised Comforts For Soldiers And Sailors procession took place at South Elmsall on Saturday, 10 July, to augment Mrs Warde-Aldam's fund for the provision of shirts, socks etc. Several hundreds of school children took part, and all the religious denominations were represented.

On Monday, 19 July, at the West Riding Assizes in Leeds, before Mr Justice Rowlett, 24-year-old miner, Walter Marriott, of 12 Wortley Street, Barnsley, was indicted for the murder of his wife, Nellie Marriott, at Barnsley, shortly after midnight on Sunday, 6 June. Mrs Marriott died as a result of a blow delivered with considerable force with a knife which entered her neck three or four inches below the left ear, and penetrated some six or seven inches vertically into the lung.

After listening to all the evidence the jury retired to consider their verdict. After a lengthy period the jury returned to ask the judge if a man who struck a blow in the heat of passion was guilty of murder.

His Lordship stated that it was murder if he struck a blow in the heat of passion, unless the passion was induced by provocation which reduced it to manslaughter. 'It must however, be provocation not only by words, but by acts,' added the Judge.

Shortly afterwards the jury found Marriott 'guilty'.

He heard the decision unmoved, but when asked if he had anything to say, exclaimed excitedly, 'I have not had fair play.'

The judge without any comment put on the black cap and pronounced the death sentence.

At Elsecar on Thursday, 29 July, the circumstances attending the death of 34-year-old Mr George Victor Davy, of Church Street, Elsecar, were inquired into. The deceased, was the youngest son of Mr John Davy, senior partner in the Elsecar firm of Messrs Davy Brothers, ironfounders. Mr Davy stated that for the last five years his son had been suffering from consumption. With a view to curing the disease, Mr Davy had taken his son to New Zealand, where they stayed six months, and later the deceased had spent five months in a private sanatorium at Leeds.

For the last month he had been 'bedfast'. He had always been in the habit of shaving himself, and on Tuesday afternoon (27th), about 3 pm, asked for a razor. Mr Davy was with his son and shortly went downstairs leaving an aunt in the bedroom. The aunt came downstairs about 4 pm, whereupon Mr Davy went upstairs shortly afterwards to sit with his son, where he discovered that his son had cut his throat with the razor, and was unconscious. He died about nine o'clock that same night. A verdict of 'suicide whilst temporarily insane,' was returned.

August 1915

The Stainborough Cricket Club has for upwards of forty years at feast time held two days sports. Owing to the war it was thought desirable not to hold any this year, but the happy thought occurred of holding military on one day, those taking place on Bank Holiday Monday under distinguished military and civil patronage on the Stainborough Cricket Ground. Hundreds of people gathered to witness a splendid programme presented by the 14th Battalion from Newhall Camp.

The *Barnsley Chronicle* commented in its edition on the 7 August:

'Yorkshire people are not likely to forget that last August Bank Holiday week synchronised with the first breaking of the war-storm. Many persons were away from home, and with a holiday atmosphere everywhere in the country, only gradually was it realised how portentous was the conflict into which we, as a nation were entering on the side of France and Russia. Peaple in Barnsley and elsewhere were almost dumfounded at the extraordinary swiftness with which the tragic situation developed... The Allies and particularly the British, will have the eventual advantage alike, in munitions, money and men. For this

reason they may look forward with serene confidence to final victory.'

During week commencing 9 August, the Empire was pleased to report record houses, where the world's greatest conjurer Chung Lee Soo was topping the bill. The 'wonderful magician' presented his entertainment in three parts and fairly bewildered the audience.

On the morning of Tuesday, 10 August, Barnsley murderer Walter Marriott, was executed at Wakefield Prison. W. A. Pierrepoint, assisted by Wallis, was the executioner.

Barnsley coroner Mr P.P. Maitland held an inquest later in the morning at Wakefield prison, where formal evidence was given by the governor, Captain Clements, Dr Maurice Herne, the Medical Officer and the Deputy Sheriff Mr Ernest R. Dodsworth, who stated that the execution was properly and promptly carried out, and that death was immediate. The coroner stated that Marriott had left a written note in his cell expressing thanks to the prison officials, especially the chaplain, wishing them all good luck. He asked God to reward every one of them from the lowest to the highest. The jury expressed themselves satisfied that sentence of death had been properly carried out.

The annual Musical Hospital Festival was held on the afternoon of Sunday, 15 August, at Grimethorpe, in the Institute cricket field. Probably owing to the threatening weather the attendance was not so large as in previous years. There was a procession through the village headed by the South Hiendley Brass Band, in which the children of the various Sunday schools, members of Friendly Societies, the Ambulance Corps and the Fire Brigade took part.

At Wombwell on Saturday, 21 August, an effort was made in aid of the movement for the provision of a Wombwell and District Motor Ambulance, fully equipped, for service at the front. The event took the form of a procession, sports and gala and raised the impressive sum of £140.

Glorious weather favoured the

HE SECOND GALA
IN AID OF
Beckett Hospital,
WILL BE HELD ON
FEAST MONDAY,
August 23rd, 1915,
AT THE
Barnsley Football Ground,
Oakwell.

August 1915
5th
Warsaw was captured from the Russians and occupied by German forces.

8th
The Turkish Battleship *Barbarousse-Hairedine* was sunk by British submarine 'E.-11' in the Dardanelles.

10th
German airship 'L.-12' was extensively damaged by British aircraft off Ostend.

13th
HMT *Royal Edward* was sunk in the Aegean by a German submarine.

19th
The German battle cruiser *Moltke* was torpedoed by British submarine 'E.-1' in the Gulf of Riga.

British submarine 'E.-13' was attacked by German warships while aground in Danish waters.

British SS *Arabic* was sunk by a German submarine.

HMS *Baralong* (special service ship) destroyed German submarine 'U.-27'.

21st
The first authenticated case of a German submarine firing on a ship's crew in open boats (British SS *Ruel*) was reported.

57th annual show on Thursday, 26 August, held under the auspices of Penistone Agricultural, Horticultural, and Floral Society. The large number of entries for the various categories were a record and huge crowds flocked to the event.

The Low Valley and District Garden Protection Society held their annual cottage garden show on Saturday, 28 August. The event was well-attended and some highly deserving prizes were given out for the remarkably high quality and varied display of locally grown vegetables, fruit and flowers, which must certainly prove to be greatly encouraging and inspirational for people to grow their own produce.

September 1915

On Wednesday, 1 September 1915, an inquest was held at Barnsley Town Hall on the body of 8-month-old John Henderson Summons, the illegitimate child of bricklayer's labourer James Henderson and Laura Summons, of 21 Cooper Street, Barnsley. The evidence moved the coroner, Mr P.P. Maitland to remark that the parents ought to be locked up and he hoped they would be punished. However, the matter might be left in the hands of the NSPCC, said Mr Maitland.

Inspector Chappell of the NSPCC stated that he had repeatedly warned Henderson and Summons to give better attention to the deceased baby. The jury returned a verdict that 'John Henderson Summons died from tubercular meningitis, following tubercular peritonitis, caused or accelerated by the very grave neglect on the part of the mother and father he was living with.'

After being severely censured by the coroner during the inquest, at its close Henderson and Summons were arrested and on the following day, Thursday, 2 September, appeared at Barnsley Borough Court before Councillor Chappell and Lieutenant Plumpton. They were charged that they unlawfully and wilfully did neglect certain children under the age of sixteen years, namely Florence Summons aged one year and ten months and John Henderson Summons aged eight months. Both prisoners pleaded not guilty. Laura Summons carried the child Florence Summons in her arms.

Inspector Chappell said he had the defendants under observation for a year and on one particular occasion had insisted that the mother take the

British wounded from the Battle of Loos in the main street of Vermelles.

child, Florence Summons, to the Beckett Hospital to have
her eyes treated, which she did but only under pressure. The
deceased child, John Henderson Summons, was healthy at
birth but his condition had deteriorated considerably during
his short life. Inspector Chappell said he had remonstrated
time after time with the parents but to no avail. He added,
that in fact they had gone from bad to worse. Asked if
they had anything to say, Henderson and Summons simply
blamed each other. The chairman, Councillor Chappell, in
addressing the prisoners said in view of the sharp sentences
which had been meted out recently the bench had thought they had got
to the bottom of this evil, but apparently that was not the case. He told
them that their conduct had been disgraceful and sentenced them to
three months in prison each, with hard labour.

The 11th annual show of fruit, flowers and vegetables in connection

> **September 1915**
> **25th**
> The Battle of Loos
> began.
>
> **30th**
> Lord Derby assumed
> control of recruiting in
> Great Britain.

with Shafton Village Working Men's Club, was held on Monday, 27 September, the number of entries totalled 280, and advance of 50 on the last year. The quality of the exhibits was excellent, fruit and celery being very prominent.

October 1915

Barnsley's recently completed Alhambra, built at a prominent site on the corner of Doncaster Road with New Street, opened its doors for public scrutiny as a first-class variety theatre on Monday, 4 October, with a programme in every way worthy of this magnificent building. Proposals to build the Alhambra were first conceived in 1910, and delays to bring the project to completion resulted in the building not being ready to open until the height of hostilities were underway. This large theatre, with a seating for 2,362 patrons in stalls and three balconies, was built to the designs of architect P.A. Hinchcliffe. The theatre having being officially opened a few days earlier, on Friday by Countess Fitzwilliam, followed by a concert for the benefit of the Incorporated Soldiers' and Sailors' Help Society. Major Carrington, on behalf of the directors received the Countess, who was accompanied by Miss Watson. The party from Wentworth Woodhouse included her ladyship's daughters, Lady Elfrida, Lady Joan and Lady Donatia. The countess was present by the architect of the Alhambra, Mr P.A. Hinchcliffe with a gold key.

Countess Fitzwilliam was presented with a bouquet of flowers by Miss Carrington. In one of the boxes was Lady Beaumont and a party from Carlton Towers. In another box were Mr and Mrs Scott-Smith, of Banks Hall. Others in the audience were the Countess of Wharncliffe and her party from Wortley Hall, Mr and Ms Fullerton, of Noblethorpe Hall, Sir Thomas and Lady Pilkington, of Chevet Park, Miss Spencer-Stanhope, of Cannon Hall, the Mayor and Mayoress of Barnsley (Hon Colonel and Mrs W.G. England), Major and Mrs Carrington, Captain McKenna, Lieutenants Hickson, Ryan and Foers, Mrs Hewitt (wife of Lieutenant-Colonel Hewitt) and party, Miss Fountain, of Birthwaite Hall, Mrs Warde-Aldam, of Frickley Hall, and party and Mrs J. Howard Taylor.

GRAND,

RECUITING RALLY.

Saturday, Oct. 2nd,

Meetings will be held at

Penistone,
1 o'clock.
Chairman, Lieut.-Col. W. L. B. HIRST V.D.

Cawthorne.
3 o'clock.
Chairman, E, M. S. PILKINGTON, Esq.

Barnsley
(In the Wholesale Fruit Market), 5-30 p.m.
Chairman, THE MAYOR, Hon. Colonel W. G. England, J.P.

Other Speakers :— Colonel RALEY, Major CARRINGTON, Capt. BURY. Capt. HUGGARD, Lieut. PLUMPTON, J.P., Ald J. S. ROSE, J.P., Dr. WILSON, J.P.; and other gentlemen.

The Mayor of Barnsley and Colonel Hirst will speak at all the above Meetings.

The Band of the Y. & L. Regt., from Pontefract, will play National and Patriotic Music. Volunteers, Home Defence Corps, and Boy Scouts are invited to attend and assist at all the Meeting. Navy, Army, and Territorial Recruiting Sergeants will be present.
BY ORDER.

GOD SAVE THE KING.
1799

ALHAMBRA. BARNSLEY.

The *Barnsley Chronicle* wrote:

'The Countess Fitzwilliam wore evening dress, and a cloak of crushed strawberry colour trimmed with ermine, and she also wore a magnificent diamond tiara. The countess is always to the fore in efforts organised for charitable purposes or for the helping of our brave soldiers and sailors, but she was particularly interested on Friday night, for her three beautiful daughters took part in a very effective tableaux which concluded the programme. Some very beautiful gowns were to be seen, but the principal interest was centred on the countess and Baroness Beaumont. The attitude of all present, however, was thoroughly in keeping with the spirit of the times.'

The opening programme for scrutiny by the wider public was in every way worthy of this magnificent building. Heading the bill for the opening week was one of England's favourite artistes, Miss Victoria Monks, known to everybody as 'John Bull's girl'. No expense was spared in the construction of the Alhambra and the management were keen to point out that the same policy will be adopted to the quality of the 'turns'.

Opening on Monday, 11 October, at the Theatre Royal, to the delight of the large audiences was a delightful Egyptian musical comedy *Sheba*. Undoubtedly something new, lavishly mounted and tastefully dressed, with weird, fascinating and fantastic effects. The initial scene opens out in the Market Square of Cairo, the city where to-day thousands of our brave soldiers are located, and the audience were introduced to the picturesque surroundings and the quaint mannerisms of the natives. Scene number two portrays the pyramids and thence to the banks of the River Nile; onward the audience is figuratively taken to the entrance of the Sheik's harem in all its splendour. Throughout, the plot is strong and interesting and brimful of exhilarating humour. *Sheba* is undoubtedly one of the most successful musical comedy revues to have visited Barnsley for a long time.

On Tuesday, 19 October, Lord Derby met the members of parliament Recruiting Committee and the Joint Labour Recruiting Committee. And with them he discussed the plan of the recruiting campaign. In the evening, at London's Mansion House, he addressed an important gathering of London mayors, chairmen of Urban District Councils in the London district, and Parliamentary agents in the metropolis upon his new recruiting scheme for the purpose of enlisting their co-operation.

His Lordship described his task as one of the most difficult problems of the country: 'Look where we were a year ago. Was not this enough to show the gravity of the situation. A look at the map seems to be a sufficient answer to those who have not yet seemed to realise what the position is. I say this is in no spirit of pessimism. I am certain that in the end all will come right.'

It transpired during the lengthy address that the secret of the success of his scheme was not an unimaginable number of recruits in the first instance, but to get so many that one might look forward with confidence to being able to supply Lord Kitchener with what he wanted, not only for his immediate requirements but for many months to come. The national register gave him the information which he required for the purpose. He wanted to get every man who could be spared, and by 'starring' men he was able to eliminate from the canvasses men who, though of military age, were encouraged on munitions or other work essential for the trade of the country. If enlistment came up to expectation, it might be that the war would be over before the older men were called upon. This was the last effort on behalf of the voluntary service. It was an appeal to the people to recruit for the people, and he hoped it would not be in vain. He was not respondent of the result if the heart of the country was touched.

A public meeting was held on the evening of Wednesday, 20 October, at the Town Hall, Hoyland, for the purpose of receiving reports of the past year's working of the township's War Distress Committee and the state of its finances. The attendance was very disappointing. Mr Nathanial Mell, the chairman, gave a review of the year's work and stated 345 cases had been dealt with, showing that this meant about 1,700 people had received assistance from the Fund. A statement showed that during the year about £1,037 had been received, excepting a contribution of £60 from the Elsecar Colliery Workmen's Fund, by donations from the four wards of this amount (using round figures) £439 had been sent to the Prince of Wales' National Relief Fund, £543 had been expended in local relief, including £50 granted to the Hoyland Silkstone Workmen's Relief Fund, to supplement a temporary deficiency, and there was at the end of August, a balance in hand of £44.

On Friday, 22 October, an habitual offender, described at Barnsley West Riding Court, as a 'pest to Dodworth', was given the maximum penalty of six-months' imprisonment with hard labour. Edward Marshall a middle-aged labourer of no fixed abode, was sent to gaol for an aggravated assault on a 16-year-old girl who was in service in Westgate, Barnsley. It was revealed in court that the scoundrel had a very bad record and had been to gaol repeatedly for interfering with women and young girls.

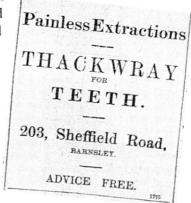

Evidence was given to the effect that the girl was walking to Dodworth on the evening of Tuesday, 19 October, and when near the borough boundary she overtook Marshall who asked her what time it was. She said it was a quarter to six, and walked on. When she had reached the railway bridge he came up to her and caught hold of her by the body. She screamed, whereupon he struck her with a cudgel (which was produced to the court). The girl fell to the ground and Marshall ran away. Afterwards the girl went to Dodworth police station and gave information to the duty officer. Marshall was found guilty as charged and sentenced.

On Saturday, 30 October, the Worsbrough and District Ambulance and Home Nursing Division kept 'Our Day' by the sale of flags and street collections in aid of the St John Ambulance Brigade and the Red Cross Society, raising the impressive sum of £36 10s.

November 1915

On the night of Wednesday, 3 November, a motor-bus fatality occurred in Barnsley, near the Junction Hotel in Doncaster Road. The unfortunate victim was 46-year-old miner, Joseph Markham, who lived at 26 Station Road, Wombwell. Mr Markham received such severe injuries that he died whilst being conveyed from the scene of the accident to the Beckett Hospital. It was a fine evening and there was no fog. It was about nine o'clock when a witness said he saw Mr Markham in the road, and as the deceased apparently saw two motor buses coming from the direction of Stairfoot, and he stepped back to let them pass. Unfortunately in doing so, Mr Markham inadvertently stepped in front of Mr Watson's motor bus which was going downhill. At the subsequent inquest held before coroner Mr P.P. Maitland, the driver of the motor bus was completely exonerated. The jury returned a verdict of 'accidentally killed by being knocked down by a motor omnibus through stepping back, apparently to avoid two other motor buses going uphill.'

On Saturday, 13 November, the *Barnsley Chronicle* informed the Barnsley public at large:

'Profound regret will be expressed throughout Barnsley and district at the news which we-today impart concerning the command of the 1st Barnsley Battalion, Lieutenant Colonel J. Hewitt having reluctantly been compelled to resign the responsible position, which he has, from the battalion's inception, held with so much distinction. Inability to physically withstand the strain of an overseas campaign is the primary cause of the Lieutenant-Colonel taking the step, and if only on this account the regret of his fine body of men will be accentuated, whilst the public of Barnsley and neighbourhood – the hundreds of parents and relatives

Lieutenant-Colonel Joseph Hewitt (1865-1923) of Ouslethwaite Hall, was a well-known and highly esteemed Barnsley solicitor, who held extensive interests in coal mining. He was raiser, and commander for one year of the 13th Barnsley Battalion, before relinquishing his command on health grounds; continuing thereafter to serve Barnsley in his legal capacity and on military at tribunals. For advice rendered to the Coal Controller during the conflict he was knighted in 1919 and subsequently created a baronet on 15 January 1921.

of those who constitute the Battalion – will join in the expression of sympathy. To Lieutenant-Colonel Hewitt, lays the indisputable honour of forming a battalion of "locals" who have won the encomiums of the high military officials, who from time to time have inspected them, as well as the golden opinions of every resident in this populous district who at one period had repeated opportunities of scrutinising the Pals and noting, as the weeks and months went by, how wonderfully improved they became in the deportment so essential for the important task which probably in the near future awaits them.

It will be recalled that in the early stages of the war Lieutenant-Colonel Hewitt cast aside his professional calling and sacrificed the whole of his time in his strenuous endeavours to place Barnsley to the forefront in securing men to form a battalion to serve His Majesty King George and his government... the number [of men] was quickly obtained, and the distinction of having raised a battalion of men whose all round fitness would bear comparison with any newly-recruited troops in the land, fell to Barnsley.

Lieutenant-Colonel Hewitt stuck as tenaciously to the battalion from the day of inception as he had done since the War Office officially placed him in command... the strain has told upon his hitherto strong constitution, and the Lieutenant-Colonel has now considered it incumbent upon him to relinquish command...'

On Wednesday, 17 November, a 3½-year-old boy, William Lapper, whose home was at 11 Low Lane, Blacker Hill, died in the Beckett

Hospital. An inquest was held before coroner Mr P.P. Maitland at the hospital the following morning. The boy's mother Maria Lapper, wife of William Lapper, miner, said her son was a healthy boy. It transpired during the proceedings that the little boy had come running into the kitchen at about 1.30 pm. The next door neighbour, Sarah Tazzyman was present as she had come to borrow a bucket of hot water. She put the bucket of hot water by the door while she refilled the copper, and shortly heard the bucket tip over and the little boy scream. He was lying on the floor, the hot water having scalded him. The boy's father went to fetch Dr Barclay Wiggins of Hoyland, who came straight away and dressed the child's injuries before the patient was taken to Beckett Hospital, where his condition gradually deteriorated. Having rallied a little, bronchial pneumonia set it and death soon followed.

A very large number of musical-loving people flocked to the Public Hall on the night of Monday, 22 November, when the Barnsley Male Voice Choir gave a concert in aid of the 1/5 York and Lancaster Regiment, who were doing such good work at the Front. The singing of the choir could not be too highly praised. They did well in all their part songs, when the harmonious blending of voices was particularly pleasing.

December 1915
In the lead up to the festive season, it was noted that the new restrictions in regard to drinking facilities in the West Riding were being sorely felt by those engaged in the licensing trade, and in conversation with several gentlemen who held liquor licences in Barnsley a representative of the *Barnsley Chronicle* was assured that all license holders consider the latest action on the part of the Control Board as altogether unreasonable. One licensee averred that his takings had depreciated by 5 per cent and that he knew of others who were equally hard hit. A beer-house keeper in a populous part of Barnsley said that it is impossible for the business done in the short period of opening – no matter how busy he might be – to compensate for the many hours he is compelled to close.

On Wednesday, 1 December, at the House of Commons a meeting of Yorkshire MPs was held to receive a deputation from the Yorkshire district of the Licensed Victuallers' National Defence League on the subject of the new drink order for the West Riding. Mr O'Grady MP, presided, and the other members present were Sir Joseph Walton, Sir G.S. Robertson, Mr F.W. Jowett, Mr R.H. Barran, Mr Samuel Roberts, Mr A.H. Marshall, Mr Major Bowden, Mr E.R. Turton and Mr O. Partington.

It was agreed on behalf of the deputation that there was a very strong feeling, not only among members of the trade, but throughout the industrial classes, that the Board of Control was acting beyond the limits suggested during the progress through the House of Commons of the measure under which it was constituted. The Board, it was suggested, was converting into a national scheme of compulsory control powers which were only intended to apply to certain areas where munitions were either produced or transported or where troops were assembled. The deputation strongly urged on the members the desirability of facilities being given for a full debate in the House of Commons. They also asked that the Board of Control should be requested to print a record of evidence taken in each area in which

[COPY.]

MESSRS. THE BARNSLEY BREWERY Co.
(LIMITED).

Agent—Mr. Jenkinson, 251, Park Road, Barnsley.

DEAR SIR,—
30th November, 1915.

THE LIQUOR TRAFFIC CONTROL BOARD ORDER.
TO SELL LIQUOR ON CREDIT IS FORBIDDEN.

To conform to the above rule we are unable to accept your order as previously. Now, it is necessary that you should forward same through the post accompanied by a cash remittance.
By selling for cash we are able to revise our price list as follows, including War Tax charge.

CASK ALE.

Gallons.	X	XX	XXX	XXXX	B.B.
9	12/-	13/6	16/-	16/9	16/9
12	16/-	18/-	21/3	22/6	22/6
18	24/-	27/-	32/-	33/6	33/6

BOTTLED ALES.

Imperial Pints, Beer and Stout	3/2 per dozen.
Do. Half-Pints Pale Ale	2/3
Do. do. Bass'	2/7
Do. do. Guinness'	2/4

Minimum quantities Pints, 4 doz.; ½-pints, 6 doz.

WINES AND SPIRITS

Proprietory brands Special Whiskies, 4/9 per bottle.
Our own Special Blends—Irish, Scotch, and Rum, 4/-.
Gin, 3/6 per bottle.
Port Wine and Sherry ... 2/- and 2/6 per bottle.

We guarantee each and every article quoted to be of the highest standard of excellence. Any article not approved within seven days will be exchanged. While thanking you for past favours we respectfully solicit your continued patronage.

Yours Faithfully,
THE BARNSLEY BREWERY CO., LTD.,
A. JENKINSON, Agent.

they based the issue of their order. A discussion took place, lasting over an hour and the deputation withdrew after thanking the MPs for their courteous reception.

The annual meeting of the Stainborough, Dodworth and District Rifle Club, at the Strafford Arms, Stainborough, was well attended and has during the past year done a good job and patriotic work by allowing free access to the range, rifles etc, for the battalions and others from Barnsley and district.

The Chairman, Mr Symonds, said he was pleased at the large assembly which was gratifying under the circumstances, numerous members connected with the club having joined the colours (a remark which led to a spontaneous burst of applause). No doubt those who had been members and associates of the club and were now serving their king and country fully realised the value of that connection. The club, he said had seventy-one members, and in addition there are fifteen members serving under the colours. During the season ten matches were shot in the Barnsley and District Rifle Association, five being won and five lost. The shootings in the competitions have been keen. The rifles and equipment were in good order, and during the past winter and early part of the season the Barnsley battalions and the Barnsley Home Defence Corps have made good use of the range.

On Friday, 3 December, at Leeds Assizes, William James Murtric, aged 43, appeared before Judge Sankey. Murtric was described a barman, of Caxton Street, Barnsley and was charged with having, whilst employed at Barnsley Post Office, stolen a postal packet on 7 August. The court heard that the prisoner had been employed as a temporary sorting clerk for nine weeks and during that time, as he subsequently admitted to an official, he had stolen six letters containing postal orders of the value of £3 13s. 6d. Mr Mellor, for the defence, said the prisoner was a married man and found it difficult to live on £1 1s. 8d., a week. His Lordship said in wartime many people were in straitened circumstances and no doubt it was not so easy to resist temptation, as it was in ordinary times. Murtric was given a sentence of six-months' imprisonment with hard labour.

On Friday, 10 December, at Barnsley West Riding Court, before Mr E.G. Lancaster (in the chair) and Mr W. Duston, Joseph Evans, miner, was summoned for stealing a dead pheasant, value 3s. 6d, the property of Captain Wentworth. He pleaded guilty. According to Mr Rideal, who prosecuted, the defendant was acting as a beater at a shoot in Barrel Wood, Thurgoland on 13 November. During the morning a bird which was shot was handed over to him but instead of him putting the pheasant along with the other dead birds, he kept it in his possession. In the evening at Wentworth Castle he was paid the usual allowance and as he was going away through the park a keeper challenged him as to what he had under his waistcoat. It was found that he had the pheasant there. He had pulled its tail off, so that it would occupy less room. The defendant said to the keeper, 'I am very sorry, but I thought it would make me a nice dinner.' The bench was not asked to send Evans to gaol but really if these offences continued such punishment would be asked for in the future. Evans was fined thirty shillings. The chairman added that future cases would probably be dealt with by imprisonment.

Opening at the Theatre Royal on Monday, 13 December, performed twice nightly and staged for six nights by Messrs Levy and Cardwell's Company's was the brilliant up-to-date revue *Well I Never,* or *Thumbs Up.* The revue was described as being charming in the extreme and the splendid audiences who attended the theatre that week were delighted, as many of the artistes who appeared in the revue were well-known to Barnsley audiences, notably Evelyn Major, Peggy McDonald, Lynorah Nelson and Tiny Hetty. At the Empire, Mr Will Smithson provided a 'tip-top programme', which included Poole's Myriorama, paying a welcome visit with its gorgeous scenery and electrical effects, quite up-to-date and portraying in artistic manner the greatest scenes at the Dardanelles and other thrilling episodes. At the Pavilion, Walter Kemp and Co. appeared in a Scottish comedy sketch, *Jock's Invention*, which was 'full of fun'. Tina Paynola, the lady mimic, was a big favourite. Pictures included the drama *The Stoning* and *Orang Outang*, a 'rib tickler'. At the Alhambra, the management of this increasingly popular amusement house, presented another programme of all-round excellence. Included on the bill were Nixon Grey, a rising comedian, who had some good songs and parodies, and the Brothers Horn were very amusing in a boxing sketch.

In the evening of Christmas Day, a packed gathering assembled for the annual prize distribution in connection with the Stainborough and Dodworth Rifle Club, which took place at the Strafford Arms Hotel, Stainborough. Dr Hunter, of Dodworth presided. The chairman eulogised the benefits which the Rifle Club afforded to men, particularly during the present crisis, and said it was their proud knowledge that a number of soldiers who were now fighting their battles owed their good marksmanship to the training they had received at Stainborough.

The return of the Barnsley battalions to Salisbury plains was the outstanding feature of Christmastide in the County Borough. When the Barnsley battalions left Silkstone Camp for fresh training quarters at Cannock Chase last summer the scenes enacted in the streets of Barnsley as the troops wended their way to the railway station were enthusiastic to a degree. But that demonstration of unbounded enthusiasm was simply nothing as compared with the scenes on Saturday night – Christmas Day – when the Barnsley Pals returned to Salisbury Plains after spending a four days furlough at home. Market Hill, Eldon Street, Cheapside and May Day Green, were never so packed with human beings in the history of the borough. Orders had been given for the 13th Service Battalion to parade on Market Hill at 10pm. The men of the 14th Service Battalion assembled at the same hour on May Day Green. The density of the crowd prohibited any organised procession of the troops, and finally the men moved off to Court House Station in sections, surrounded by their friends and loved ones. In other respects the greatest of all festivals was spent much on the usual lines. Shopkeepers admitted that trade was as good, and in some cases far better than it had ever been at 'cheer' at home, others less fortunate were being well looked after. For instance treats given to patients and inmates of the Beckett Hospital, Lundwood Hospital, Kendray Hospital and Union Workhouse were on a lavish scale. 736 invitations were extended to participate in the 30th annual old folks' treat given on Christmas Day in the Regent Street School. Over 500 elderly residents sat down to a sumptuous spread, which was followed by splendid entertainment.

The evacuation of Gallipoli underway.

The legacy left by Mr George Pitt, a Barnsley benefactor, in 1865, the distribution of which taking place every two years, enabled 420 old Barnsley 'deserving poor' to receive welcome Christmas gifts. On this occasion, £65 12s.6d. (worth £6,830.38 in 2016) was distributed, in amounts varying from 6s. (£31.22 in 2016) to 2s.6d. (£13.01 in 2016). All the recipients were over 60 years of age. Two were aged 90, thirty-four from 80 to 89 years, 181 from 70 to 79 years and 202 from 60 to 69 years. The varying sums being distributed according to the needs of the individual cases.

At the Theatre Royal during the last week of December *Kismet* proved to be an intensely popular attraction, the theatre enjoying splendid houses all week. The scene is laid in the Baghdad of *The Arabian Nights*, and each of the scenes was full of interest and enjoyment for the appreciative audiences. The delightful musical comedy *Find the Lady*, proved to be a splendid and successful holiday attraction at the Empire. Presenting its first Christmas season the recently opened Alhambra drew big crowds throughout the entire week, where Wee Georgie Wood scored a great success, in the first half of the week with *Winkles* and in the second half he presented an entirely new turn *Jim's Pal*, in which he was equally successful. Mr Wood's undoubted talents were augmented by a splendid and varied array of performances, including Thora, a clever ventriloquist with original ideas of mystifying the audience, the Three Brothers Huxter, acrobats, were greatly admired and Cosgrove and Burns, the crazy vocalists were very amusing. The management of this new, large and opulent theatre, eager to start the New Year well, were successful in securing at enormous expense, the celebrated English illusionist, Oswald Williams, and an impressive line up of vaudeville attractions.

On Friday, 31 December, at Barnsley West Riding Court, before Alderman Herne, Mr H.J. Broomhall and Mr J. Cauldwell, 11-year-old Horace Sykes of Stairfoot, was charged on remand of stealing 1s. 8 ½d. in cash, the stolen money belonging to Harriet Hirst. The offence was admitted, and Police Constable Bell proved the case. It was pointed out that only a few weeks previously the lad was before the court on a charge of housebreaking and was birched. The boy's father said the lad was absolutely beyond control. There had been several complaints about him. The defendant was ordered to be sent to an industrial school until he attained the age of sixteen.

Mitchell Main Colliery. Old Barnsley

Chapter Four

1916: Over the top

January 1916

The circumstances surrounding the death of 15-year-old pony-driver, Thomas Boocock Bullett, of 105 Barnsley Road, Wombwell was the subject of an inquest held at Wombwell before coroner P.P. Maitland on the afternoon of Monday, 17 January 1916. The deceased boy worked as a pony driver at Mitchell Main Colliery and was killed just as he was about to leave work on the afternoon shift on Friday, 14 January. He was described as a very intelligent, well-beloved boy with an ambition to get on in the world. Present at the inquest were Mr Mottram, junior (HM Inspector of Mines), Mr J. W. Halmshaw (manager of the Mitchell Main Colliery), Mr J.G. Beardsall (under-manager) and Mr Flint (Yorkshire Miners' Association).

The deceased boy's father Mr John Henry Boocock, said that his son had worked at the Mitchell Main Colliery for four or five months and was previously employed at Houghton Main. He liked his work at Mitchell Main and never complained. About midday on Friday he left home for work and was brought home dead at about 10.30 that night.

Arthur Walker, 'rope boy' [haulage lad], of 83 Blythe Street, Wombwell, said the deceased passed him with his pony at about 9.30 pm. That was at the landing and the deceased was walking between the full and empty road. The witness said at the time he was taking a tail rope off a train of full corves (wagons). He took the rope off and hung the end of it on to a prop. When asked how long the rope was the witness said he had no idea but added that it was a very long one. The prop was about 6 feet long and supported a bar. Having fastened the prop witness rapped four times to communicate with the engineman. That signal was for the rope to be tightened so as to keep it out of the way of corves. The rope tightened, the work of a second or two. When efficiently tightened witness signalled 'one' as usual. He let go the wires and the rope gave a jerk. The prop broke and flew towards the bottom where the deceased had gone. The prop broke at its middle where Arthur Walker had fastened it. The rope was not to be seen after the prop had gone.

Subsequently he saw the rope coiled up 20 yards away. Arthur Walker said at first he jumped aside for safety, and when the dust had cleared he followed on to see what was up. He first came across half the prop about six yards away. It was the top half as the lower half had remained in situ. The prop was laid in the middle of the full road. Six yards farther on he found the deceased, lying on his back between the two roads. He seemed to be dead and there was a lot of blood just underneath his head. The deceased's pony was found 150 or 200 yards farther on. The rope was found about 10 yards beyond the body. Arthur Walker said he did not hear any shout or cry. He went for assistance and found Robert Turnbull, the corporal. More assistance was obtained.

The manager of Mitchell Main Colliery, Mr J.W. Halmshaw, produced a portion of the broken prop and said there was nothing on the outside to indicate that it was a bad one. Now that it was broken he could see that it was slightly hollow inside. The rope must have been very tight to break the prop. Either the rope was tightened by the engine or it might have snagged and caught the endless rope going up, but the latter was not probable.

The next witness produced was Robert Turnbull, 'pit corporal' of 10 Pearson's Field, Wombwell, who appeared in his 'pit muck,' having just finished his shift. He said when the accident occurred he was down looking after some of the boys. The engineman in this instance was under him. Mr Turnbull said he was not in a position to say whether the signal was given or not. He had never at the end of a shift seen the rope fastened to a run of full tubs. He had seen it fastened to a bar and prop. When questioned concerning James Guest, Mr Turnbull said Guest had various times for leaving the pit.

There was an interruption to the proceedings before the next witness arrived: 25-year-old Richard Crow, a 'corporal', residing at 157 Barnsley Road, Wombwell, who caused a considerable delay having arrived at the inquest at the end of his shift. He said he worked against Guest for some hours on the day of the fatal accident. The witness said that he usually heard the signals. He did that afternoon but heard none during the evening. They might have been given without his knowing it. When Guest brought the last load up he asked 'Could he finish?' and Crow said he told Guest that he could go home then. That was about 9.15. Crow said he heard of the accident when Arthur Walker came to him about 9.30 and said the boy was bleeding to death. Crow said he sent for an ambulance and went there. Crow said it was perfectly usual to leave a rope round a set of tubs at night and added that he heard the rope 'come' but he did not think anything of it at the time. The coroner remarked that this was very strange.

In addressing the jury the coroner remarked:

> *'There is no doubt that some of the witnesses are not telling the truth. And as long as you have witnesses who do not tell the truth you cannot come to any definite result. It seems to me on the face of it that the only thing you can do is to return an open verdict.'*

The coroner, Mr Maitland, then asked if the jury would agree to that or did they wish him to adjourn the inquest? Only one hand went up in favour of an adjournment. The coroner having characterised the evidence as very unsatisfactory, an open verdict was returned.

On Monday, 17 January, a married couple from Worsbrough Bridge, colliery labourer Alfred Turton and his wife, Betsy, were in the dock at Barnsley West Riding Court, charged with neglecting their four younger children, aged 15, 13, 11 and 7, respectively. The Bench was chaired by G.H. Norton. Also sitting were Alderman Rose and W.L. Wadsworth.

Police Constable Hyde said that on 12 January accompanied by Sergeant Brown, he had visited the defendant's house, which was in a filthy and neglected condition. The children were also in a neglected condition. Not only were they verminous , but they were suffering with sore heads and were all without exception, badly clad. The youngest boy, 11-year-old Willie, was very emaciated and weighed only 3st, 9lbs. He was nothing 'but skin and bone', and every bone in his body could be seen protruding through his thin skin.

Constable Hyde then went on to describe the conditions in which the Turton family were living. He said the living room was badly furnished and very dirty, and there was only a bucketful of coal in the entire house. In the sparsely furnished front bedroom, there was an iron bedstead and two straw mattresses, which were in a filthy condition. There was no bedding in any of the three bedrooms and there was an appalling stench.

Evidence was then provided concerning the Turton family's finances. Alfred Turton's weekly wage averaged 35s. (equivalent to £162.34 in 2016). With the money contributed to the weekly budget by the Turtons' two eldest sons the defendants had £3.10s.0d. (equivalent to £212.85 in 2016) coming in each week. The rent amounted to 4s.6d. (equivalent to £20.87 in 2016), leaving the not inconsiderable sum of £3.5.6d. (equivalent to £303.80 in 2016) a week with which to run the household. During the evidence it transpired that Alfred Turton worked regularly but was a heavy drinker at weekends. However, Betsy Turton was said to be continually under the influence of drink.

Dr Beverley said that the defendants' son, Willie, weighed 1½ stones less than could be reasonably expected and that he was satisfied that the boy's condition arose from a state of semi-starvation. Mr J.K. Lee, for the defence cross-examined the doctor and said he believed Willie Turton to be suffering from tubercular peritonitis, which would account for his condition. However, Dr Beverley disputed this. The doctor went on to say that two sons who were working and two younger sons, all slept in one bed in which there was scarcely a dry patch. The bed in which the defendants slept was verminous. Dr Beverley concluded his evidence by saying that the condition of the children was entirely due to neglect.

Mr Lee then called two of the older children to give evidence. Jack Turton, aged 19, and Martha Jane Turton, aged 15, in their evidence maintained they had plenty of food and clothing, and that the dirty condition of the younger children was as a result of them playing with children from other families. They had attended school regularly, with the exception of Willie, who had been ill for the last eighteen months, and couldn't keep his food down. Mr Lee then produced Willie and his younger sister and handed in a certificate from Dr Fryer, which stated that Willie was suffering from tubercular peritonitis. He then went on to say that the police evidence was mainly concerned with the dirty state of the children and the weakness of the boy Willie; and with regard to Willie, the certificate from Dr Fryer showed the boy was suffering from a type of consumption. Mr Lee concluded by saying that most of the children were old enough to keep themselves clean.

The Bench, however, were apparently unmoved and unconvinced by the proffered defence. After some discussion, the chairman, Mr Norton, said:

'This is a very bad case, indeed; it is certainly the worst I have had before me in my experience. Instead of keeping your children clean, you treated them more like savages than anything else. The condition of the house is absolutely disgusting. You have been convicted before for similar offences – in 1905, one month, and in 1911, one month. Apparently it has not had any effect. There is no excuse for dirt, and you were earning good wages. We cannot give you less than three months' imprisonment.

As the sentence was being passed, a considerable din emanated from within the courtroom. Alfred and Betsy Turton's children were all present, including a married daughter and a grown-up daughter and son.

Without exception, from the youngest to the eldest sibling, they all burst into loud crying and sobbing.

An 11-year-old Worsbrough Bridge boy, James Tordoff, found himself in the dock at Barnsley West Riding Court, on Wednesday, 19 January 1916, charged with indulging in the dangerous practice of riding on the back of tramcars. Mr J. Raley, prosecuting on behalf of the Barnsley Traction Company, said that this was the first case of its kind to be brought by the company and it was fervently hoped that there would be no further necessity for proceedings. Concern was expressed about mischievous children, jumping on the back of tramcars, and whilst holding the rail, riding considerable distances. The court heard that as a result of this practice one boy had been killed and another injured. In wartime Britain, since it had become necessary to employ lady conductors on the cars youngsters had been taking advantage in order to indulge in what they considered to be great fun. In the case in question, young James Tordoff had only been prevented from serious injury by the timely intervention of a police constable, who caught the boy as he released his hold of the rail and fell. To emphasise the seriousness of the case and in the hope it would deter others, the youngster was given a fine of 10s. (Worth £46.38 today)

At the Theatre Royal for the week commencing Monday, 24 January,

A view looking up High Street, Worsbrough Dale, showing Tramcar 6, the type of car that James Tordoff took rides on. Old Barnsley

January 1916
27th
Conscription was introduced in Great Britain.

Mr Alfred Sultro's masterpiece *The Walls of Jericho*, was enjoyed by large crowds. This powerful play gripped the audience throughout. A full variety programme could be seen at the Alhambra, where audiences concurred there was not a poor turn appearing. At the Empire Mr Percy Honri presented his 1916 Revue, and it was judged by the audience to be a great success. At the Pavilion, 'The Seeners', the great Russian troupe of whirlwind dancers and singers, direct from the London Opera House, topped the bill.

On 29 January, the *Barnsley Chronicle* were pleased to announce: 'The first batch of tobacco and cigarettes sent off under the *Barnsley Chronicle* Tobacco Fund have reached their destination and already acknowledgements have arrived in Barnsley and neighbourhood from grateful recipients.'

Mr J. Allatt, the secretary of the Grimethorpe Sunday School, in presenting his annual report, stated that the past year had been the most prosperous year on record. There was an increase in both scholars and teachers. Mr Allatt commented, 'We have started a system of giving out the average attendance for each Sunday and so far it has proved beneficial. We have had the misfortune to lose three of our scholars through death, and one teacher is on active service, but we were pleased of his presence during the Christmas holidays, and we pray that God will watch over him. On New Year's Day we had our annual prize distribution and tea. Mr D. Toone officiated and spoke words of encouragement to the scholars. We had also a Christmas decorated with toys of varied description. Mr R. Gorner 'made a splendid Santa Claus', and the scholars enjoyed themselves immensely.

SMOKES FROM HOME
Barnsley Chronicle Tobacco Fund.

DELICIOUS

" **Barnsley Chronicle** " **Tobacco Fund**
(Amalgamated with the " Chronicle" Comforts Fund.)

FOR ALL SOLDIERS.

Ordinary Cost, **9/10** | Parcel and Postage for **3/-** | Special Coupon

CONTENTS OF PARCEL:—
¼-lb. United Service Tobacco, usually sold at 8d. per oz.
200 Cigarettes (Woodbines) ; Carriage 1/-. Or—

Z. —280 Wills' Woodbine Cigarettes 3/-
X. —575   Ditto   Ditto 5/-
W. —3 pounds Wills' United Service Mixture 5/-
V. —280 Wills' Gold Flake Cigarettes 5/-

A Postcard ready addressed back to you for your friend's acknowledgment is enclosed in every parcel.

One Coupon for each Parcel.

Wombwell Main Colliery. Old Barnsley

February 1916

Mr Herbert Smith presided over an important meeting of the Executive Council of the Yorkshire Miners' Association on Monday, 7 February at which the employment of female (pit-top) labour in the mining industry was raised.

It was also announced that the voting of members on the question of providing a convoy of motor ambulances for service at the front had resulted in a big majority (60,250 to 34,450) in favour of the scheme, and that the members had agreed to contribute 6d. per week for fourteen weeks, half-members to contribute half-rates.

The president, Mr Smith, said seeing that they had 27,000 members in His Majesty's service, Yorkshire was as anxious as any other county to secure for the wounded a prompt and efficient motor ambulance service. While they thought the government ought to make adequate provision, they had agreed to make contributions which they estimated would realise about £35,000.

The council received with regret the news of the death in action of forty-two more members, bringing the associations' war losses up to 673.

Consideration of what action should be taken in regard to the military service was also discussed, about which Mr Smith was moved to say:

'The association is not wishful to hamper in any way the progress of the country from a military point of view in accomplishing the defeat of German militarism. But we feel that the response that is being made to the voluntary system is meeting the nation's requirements. If it is to be conscription, then the wealthy of this country ought to be conscripted in the first instance, and every able-bodied man likewise if the necessity arises. Before men are asked to give their lives fighting on the battlefield money is required to prosecute our country's cause to a successful issue. Hence at once the necessity of at once conscripting the wealth of the country for the purpose.'

Mr Smith added that a report had been sent to the Association that female labour had that morning been introduced in the lamp-room at Nunnery Colliery (Sheffield), and that the council had passed a resolution to take up the question with the owners; and in the event of the female labour not being withdrawn at once the men would be supported in any legal action which might be taken in accordance with the rules of the Association.

Two licensees were summoned before the Barnsley West Riding magistrates on Wednesday 9th, for breaches of the Central Control Board (Liquor Order). One, was an innkeeper whose house was open for the consumption of intoxicating drink during prohibited hours, and the other was an off-licence holder who transgressed the regulation about the 'long pull' (illegal extra beer added).

William Gill Burgess, innkeeper of the Woodman Inn, Thurgoland, was summoned for having his premises open during prohibited hours. The evidence against the landlord was proven. The chairman said that two years ago Burgess was convicted for selling during prohibited hours. The Bench had carefully considered that case which he was now up for, and wished to point out that the Order was very severe. Defendant's were liable for up to six months' imprisonment or a fine of £100. This being the first case in the Staincross Division they were somewhat willing to take a lenient view, but this would not be the case if there were any more of these prosecutions. Burgess was fined £5.

Wombwell beer-retailer, George Myers, was summoned for supplying the 'long-pull'. Superintendent McDonald said at 7.15 pm on 1 February, Sergeant Shepherd saw a 7-year-old boy come out of the defendant's beer-off shop carrying a quart bottle containing beer. The sergeant asked what the boy had and the boy replied, 'A pint of beer for Mrs Lax.' Sergeant Shepherd took the beer back to the shop and measured it in the presence of the defendant. He found that the quantity of

> **February 1916**
> **21st**
> The Battle of Verdun began.

beer in the bottle exceeded a pint. A pint of beer was asked for and paid for, said Superintendent McDonald. This might not be considered a serious offence but at present the great majority of the people trading in this line conformed with the Order. It was quite easy for the police to spot the traders who were not complying with the new regulation, because those who gave the long pull now, pulled a long trade with it. The bench retired to consider the evidence presented, which was considerable, and showed beyond any doubt that the defendant habitually gave the long-pull to regular customers. On their return the chairman said they had given every attention to the case and had come to the conclusion that this had been a contravention of the Order. They did not think the case a very bad one. There had been a little too much carelessness in allowing over measure, and they hoped the defendant would be very careful in the future. This time a small penalty of £1 would be imposed.

On 10 February, at the Keresforth schools, Dodworth Road, a very successful whist drive and dance was held to raise money for the Soldiers' and Sailors' Fund, to provide 'comfort' for soldiers and sailors. Despite the inclement weather the function was very well attended.

March 1916

On 2 March, the landlord and landlady of the Lord Nelson Hotel, Shambles Street, Barnsley, Mr Henry Rowe and his wife Hannah, were found guilty as charged at Barnsley Borough Court, for selling rum contrary to the Order of the Central Control Board Area (Liquor Traffic) West Riding Area. They were each fine £5, with costs and witnesses allowances.

On Monday, 6 March, there was a meeting of the Yorkshire Miners' Association, at Barnsley. The council learned with the deepest regret of the death of fifty-one further members whilst doing military service. The latest list of casualties brought the war losses of the Association up to 724.

Commencing Monday, 6 March, the Alhambra scored something of a coup in theatrical circles when they presented one of the major attractions of the day as top of the bill, Miss Vesta Tilley (Lady de Frece)

THE ALHAMBRA, BARNSLEY

'The World-Famed Male Impersonator', in a selection of her repertoire, including The Army of to-day's all right.'

On Monday, 13 March, the precautions to be observed locally in the event of a raid by hostile aircraft formed the subject of an interesting discussion at the monthly meeting of the council at Worsbrough.

On 18 March, the building of cottage property in the area of the Darton Urban District Council continued apace. On 14 March plans for eight houses proposed to be erected in Kexborough Lane, Darton, were presented and passed. In each of these houses will be a bath, fixed in the scullery.

On 22 March, there was another licensing prosecution at Barnsley West Riding Court. George Bramall, licensee of the Station Inn,

The Station Inn, Silkstone Common.

Silkstone Common, was summoned for keeping his house open during prohibited hours. On conviction the defendant was fined £5. At the conclusion of the proceedings Superintendent McDonald, addressing the court and clearly with the intention of warning other members of the licensed trade, said (of Mr Bramall): 'I wish to give him warning that if he does not discontinue supplying drink to these people (several locals

George Bramall, licensee of the Station Inn, Silkstone Common, photographed in 1896 with four of his sons. Left to right: Albert 11 years, Horace 4 years, Frank 2 years and Eli 7 years. Albert died aged 11, sometime after this picture was taken. Horace, shown in uniform on the right, joined the Royal Navy and was killed on 22 September 1914 when his ship HMS *Aboukir* was sunk by a German submarine, *U-9*. His brother, Frank, was a private in the 2/4 Battalion Y/L. He was killed in 1917. Eli, the last surviving son had left for Australia in 1911 and joined the Australian Infantry Force in 1916, he survived the war. George himself died 18 August 1918 aged 59. Andrew Horsfield

Horace Bramall in his naval uniform.

had been fined £1 each at the same hearing), that it is my intention to report the house with a view to getting it closed for the period of the war.'

On the 30 March, at Barnsley Borough Court, before the Mayor (Alderman Holden), in the chair, Alderman Rose, and others, a number of licensing offences in connection with the Blenheim Road Working

Men's Club, were inquired into. Supplying drink during prohibited hours was at the root of the charges. Extensive evidence was presented. After consulting in private, the mayor said the Bench was absolutely unanimous in their opinion that this was a very bad case indeed. No doubt there had been a tremendous amount of laxity and carelessness in the management of the club. A badly conducted club affected the moral welfare in any neighbourhood, and the magistrates thought they could do nothing less than strike the club off the register (close it down) for twelve months. The club secretary would have to pay the costs and Samuel Cresswell, the club steward, was fined £10 (worth £927.65 in 2016).

April 1916

On 4 April, Lord Derby received a deputation from the National Union of Attested Married Men, who laid their views on the present recruiting status before him. There was a full discussion on the best methods of securing the services of all available single men. Lord Derby informed the deputation of what was being done administratively and what could be done by legislation.

> **April 1916**
> **12th**
> British forces surrendered to Turkish forces at Kut in Mesopotamia.

On the 13 April, at the Barnsley Borough Police Court, three Barnsley men were sent to prison over offences regarding stolen whisky. Frank Carr, a shunter in the employ of the Great Central Railway Company, of 10 Burton Terrace, was charged with stealing on three separate dates forty bottles of whisky, valued at £11, the property of the railway company. He pleaded guilty. Thomas William Hodson, ripper (miner), of 21 Junction Street, and James Hardman, miner, of 43 Junction Street, were all charged with 'receiving'. The mayor characterised it as a very serious case. Carr, who had been to prison before, received six months; Hardman got two months and Hodson one month.

English Flag Day.

Honour yourselves and your Countrymen at the Front by purchasing and wearing a Memento of the same on

Saturday, April 22nd, 1916.

PROCEEDS IN AID OF THE

BARNSLEY WAR LEAGUE OF HELP.

875

An extremely lively situation developed in Parliament on the eve of the Easter recess. The tension arose over the recruiting question and the attitude of Mr Asquith due to his well known declaration that he would rather go out of office than consent to a measure of general conscription.

On 27 April, the mayor (Alderman Holden), in the chair at Barnsley Borough Court, took the opportunity to voice an opinion expressed by many local people recently, when two men named Fred Wilson and George Wilkinson, were summoned for driving motor cars in a dangerous manner, and were therefore fined 40s. and 60s. respectively. The mayor sent out a clear message to irresponsible and inconsiderate motorists driving through Barnsley and districts. His worship told the court: 'We intend to stamp out this furious driving about the streets to the danger of the public. The drivers in many cases don't consider the safety of people at all but race one against another. We are determined we will put a stop to it.'

At the annual general meeting of the Beckett Hospital Saturday and Sunday Committee, held at the Town Hall, Barnsley on 28 April, reference was made by Mr Alfred Whitham (stationer) to the observations made by the mayor with reference to the furious driving of motor cars in the town and neighbourhood, reported in the *Barnsley Chronicle*, that day. Mr Witham commended the remarks delivered from the magisterial bench, saying that his Worship's remarks, would meet with the strong approval not only of the Hospital Committee but by everyone who had the welfare of the community at heart. He was pleased to read in the paper that the mayor had declared that he would do all in his power to suppress the evil and when they reflected upon the number of accidents which had occurred through this one thing they would agree that the resolve was well timed.

On the night of Saturday, 29 April, 46-year-old Private Leonard Helliwell, of the Northumberland Fusiliers, bid goodbye to his wife, Mary, of 27 Talston Rowe, Wombwell, at Barnsley railway station. Private Halliwell had been in the army for eighteen months and had obtained leave to attend the funeral of one of his sons. His parting words were, 'I will look forward to being home at Whitsuntide.' Early the following morning his mangled body was discovered on the railway line a mile from Bradbury Station near Darlington. At the inquest, in summing up the coroner said there was no evidence as to the actual nature of the accident, but there was presumptive evidence that the unfortunate soldier was travelling in a train, when by some means or other he fell on to the line. The mangled state of the body was due in all probability to injuries inflicted by a passing train. The jury returned a verdict of accidental death, caused by falling from a train on the North-Eastern Railway.

May 1916

On 2 May, at Barnsley West Riding Court, Thomas Coulson, landlord of the Royal Oak Inn, Platts Common, was summoned for supplying intoxicating liquor during prohibited hours. A customer, Alfred Adamson, was also summoned for taking the liquor from the premises during prohibited hours. The charges were brought because Mr Adamson was apprehended by two police constables shortly after 10.30 pm on Saturday, 22 April, as he left by the back door of the public house. He was found to have two bottles of beer in his possession. The chairman said the magistrates had decided to convict, and addressing Mr Coulson, said he supposed he knew he was liable to a fine of £100. The charge had been proved and they would impose a penalty to put a stop to this in future and imposed a fine of £10 on the landlord and £1 on Adamson.

BOOK THESE DATES—MAY 25, 26,

Public Hall, Barnsley.

PATRIOTIC MAY FAI

Remember the Local Lads at the Fro
Comforts Urgently Needed.

Help the Mayor to provide them.

See Later Announcements.

ALL CONTRIBUTIONS TO THE FAIR THANKFULLY RECEIV
(1020)

The 'great fair' and three days' auction sale in aid of the Mayor's Comforts Fund for Barnsley, opened on Thursday, 25 May, in the Public Hall, and on the first day the visitors expressed their amazement with the magnitude of effort that had been made. The fair was opened by Mrs W.E. Long, of Hurts Hall, Saxmundham, and this was considered a most appropriate choice, for Mrs Long being a member of the Wentworth family, who had for many years (since about 1708, in fact) been associated with every good work originating or taking place in Barnsley and district. The mayor, wearing his robes and chain of office, presided, and others present on the platform were the mayoress,

Miss Fountain, Captain Bruce Wentworth, Lieutenant-Colonel Hewitt, Alderman Rose, Alderman Rideal, Councillor Plumpton and Mr W.P. Donald (town clerk).

The opening ceremony concluded, the business of raising money at once commenced with an auction sale in which some choice goods, every one a bargain, were put up. Thursday proved to be a grand start to the fair, and the hopes created by the first day's success were realised on Friday and Saturday, the total amount raised by the effort approximating £2,000 (£159,000 in 2016), this would have been a noteworthy achievement in peace times, but under existing conditions it was little short of marvellous, and but one more example of the splendid and practical patriotism of the people of Barnsley and District.

The Barnsley tribunal (for exemption from military service) had a prolonged sitting on Monday, 29 May, when many cases were dealt with, most of the applicants being married men. The tribunal consisted of the mayor (Alderman H. Holden) in the chair, Alderman Rideal, Alderman Rose, Councillor Coterill and Councillor Bray, with Lieutenant-Colonel Hewitt (military representative) and Mr W.P. Donald (Town Clerk). One hundred and fifty-seven appeals were heard.

Among them were:

A dental mechanic who is in business for himself, appealed on personal grounds, stating that he was a married man with four children. He had a number of cases in hand which could not be completed under six months. His business was mostly a 'credit' one, and he had already accepted payment for work which he had still to do. Alderman Rideal stated: 'You will have nothing to fear against any proceedings.' The applicant replied that it was not a matter of that, but if he had to go he could not keep his house going. His appeal was refused, but he was allowed 'one month's grace'.

When the name of a certain person was called out there was no response, and Colonel Hewitt said that he did not wonder there was no appearance. The applicant was a bookmaker and commission agent and he supposed that he claimed exemption on the grounds that it was of national importance that his business should be continued and so help to win the war. The mayor said: 'I daresay you are sorry he is not here.' Colonel Hewitt remarked: 'It is not a certified occupation (laughter).' The mayor concluded: 'We are sorry he is not here.'

An adjournment of two months was granted to a taxi-cab proprietor, who pleaded that he only had one man and two boys (of seventeen) left. Their work was largely for collieries, and their cars were used by the

An exemption from military service hearing.

police in case of accidents, and they also did duty on the occasion of Zeppelin alarms.

An insurance superintendent asked for absolute exemption. This raised a comment from Colonel Hewitt: 'Yes there are lots of people who want to join the Guards but they are not open.' The man said he had tried to join the Royal Flying Corps. Colonel Hewitt replied: 'Of course you didn't go to enlist in the general service. You wanted to go in a particular unit.' The appeal was refused.

Another insurance agent asked for two months' extension, and in doing so he reminded the court that there were certain penalties under the Insurance Act. Colonel Hewitt said: 'There will be bigger penalties if the Germans come! (laughter). Appeal was refused.

'I claim to be in a reserved occupation,' said a wheelwright. He had been in the business for the last seven years and did a great deal of work for the coal merchants in and around Barnsley. He was married and had one child. The clerk asked: 'Do you employ any men?' Applicant replied: 'No Sir.' Town Clerk: 'You have a small shop and work for yourself without assistance?' Applicant: 'Yes.' The application refused but he was allowed one month's grace. Applicant protested, saying: 'But I am in a reserved occupation.' Colonel Hewitt told him: 'You have the right to appeal to Wakefield. The clerk confirmed: 'The Tribunal has considered the fact that you are in the occupation you mention, but in view of the facts of the case cannot grant the application. Applicant concluded: 'If I had gone to the Public Hall I might have got it there.'

> **May 1916 31st**
> The Battle of Jutland.

'I manage my own business,' said a pork butcher who had a wife and three children dependent upon him. He had been in business for three years for himself, nobody worked for him, and he did the killing of pigs himself. Colonel Hewitt said: 'Just the sort of man to kill Germans.' The clerk agreed: 'The same!' Appeal was adjourned for two months.

June 1916

On Monday, 5 June, the tribunal for the County Borough of Barnsley met again, when fifty applications for postponement or exemption were heard. Among these were:

A painter and paperhanger asked for exemption on domestic grounds as he had a wife and six children wholly dependent upon him and two children partially dependent, It was suggested that the case should be adjourned for the applicant to be medically examined and someone also remarked that the applicant would be out of work because the painters were on strike. Colonel Hewitt remarked: 'If this man is out of work and he can find work of national importance let him go.' The applicant said he was not out of work as he had got employment at Sheffield, but added, 'I am willing to take up work of national importance if you will let me stay at home with my family. The clerk said if the applicant could not get work he should go and see him. Colonel Hewitt said, 'Come to me I will find you work.' The mayor added: 'I would not mind working for either of you.' [Laughter]

'It is impossible for a woman to cut a joint of meat fit to send to anybody's table,' said a Sheffield Road butcher, who stated that he did his own buying, selling, and slaughtering. At the present time he was slaughtering two beasts and five sheep a week. Asked if he had been to Pontefract to be examined, he replied: 'No I have not had time. I have to look after my own business first.' Alderman Rose asked: 'Do you treat it as a joke? The applicant replied: 'Butchering is not worth much at the present time. The Clerk warned him: 'Don't make statements which might do you harm.' Appeal was refused – but he was given a period of grace.

An employer applied for a tin, zinc and sheet-iron worker who had been in his works for fifteen years. He was the only 'tinner' he had left; and if he went the applicant said he would have to close this branch of business, also stating that 'women could not do the work'; and that it was impossible to get tinners at the present time. The man had been passed for labour service at home. The mayor asked: 'Have any other tinners gone?' The applicant replied: 'The apprentice went last week. All the other eligible men I had have gone and two more are going next week.' The applicant then pointed out that formerly this occupation was

June 1916
4th
The start of the
Brusilov Offensive.

on the reserved list. Provisional exemption was granted on the understanding that the applicant did not appeal for any other men.

On the night of 8 June, a meeting in connection with the Stainborough, Dodworth and District Rifle Club was held at the Strafford Arms Hotel, Stainborough, under the presidency of Mr G.J. King. The chairman said that like all other institutions their club felt the effects of the war. They had been hit very hard, not only by the loss of the members, who had joined the colours, but they had lost their secretary and Captain, Mr W.J. Fisher, who had been called upon to do his bit, and was now in a munitions department in Glasgow. His absence placed the club in a somewhat difficult position. He hoped, however, that the club would be kept going to carry on its good training and work. Mr E. Symons was elected secretary in Mr Fisher's absence, and in accepting the office said he should be very sorry for the club to collapse and he would be pleased to do his best until Mr Fisher's return.

A.H. Longley, Adjutant to the 1st Barnsley and District Battalion West Riding Volunteers, wrote asking for the renewal of the privilege granted to the Volunteers to use the Stainborough Rifle Range, and the meeting decided to allow the use of the 50 and 100 yards ranges, on any day except Thursdays and Saturdays, the Volunteers to provide their own ammunition and target cards.

On Monday, 12 June, the choir and friends connected with Dodworth Mission church and choir visited the huts a Newhall camp and gave 'a splendid rendering of their Whitsuntide hymns.' The concert was highly appreciated by the men.

Colonel England JP, presided on the evening of Wednesday, 14 June at a meeting of the Committee of the Barnsley Patriotic Fund, held at the *Barnsley Chronicle* buildings. The fund was resuscitated in August 1914, shortly after the outbreak of the present war, and the amount of subscriptions received (in round figures) totalled £7,066. Of this, the sum of £5,616 had been paid to dependants of men serving with the 5th York and Lancaster regiments, to the dependants of Barnsley Reservists and other volunteer soldiers resident in the borough; and also the dependants of the lads who comprise the First and Second Barnsley battalions.

The wide scope of the work of this may be judged by the fact that no fewer than about 400 families (representing over 700 children) had received financial assistance weekly. Consequent upon the war having lasted much longer than was anticipated, and the fact that there were

The *Barnsley Chronicle* buildings in Peel Square. Tasker Trust

numerous applicants in consequence of the Group system coming into vogue, the committee discussed at length the new situation which had arisen. A further appeal for additional funding would be the order of the day. A certain number of firms and tradesmen subscribed with commendable regularity, and whilst the committee fully appreciated this they would have had still greater pleasure that all the masters and workmen had contributed to a Fund that is solely for the benefit of Barnsley people. It was with confidence that the committee thus made a further appeal.

July 1916

At the beginning of the month Dr F. A. Sharpe, the Medical Officer of Health, presented his report concerning housing conditions at Barnsley.

Of a total of 10,620 families or separate occupiers enumerated in the Borough, 10,570 were private families, and of these forty-four were enumerated in tenements of one room; 519 tenement in two rooms; 1,407 tenements in three rooms; 4,333 in tenements of four rooms; 2,716 in tenements of five rooms; the remaining families occupying houses having more than five rooms. The report also showed that the great majority of people in Barnsley lived in houses containing four of five rooms.

July 1916
1st
The start of the Battle of the Somme.

The report also showed that in Barnsley there were 329 houses using 185 water closets: that being a little less than 1.8 houses to one closet. In the course of his observations to the Committee, Dr Sharpe said: 'The conclusions I am bound to come to are that, firstly, there is a certain insufficiency of dwelling houses which has been relieved partly and temporarily by the enlistment of about one-tenth of our population; and secondly, that much of the accommodation provided possesses many sanitary defects of all kinds varying from those capable of easy and immediate improvement to a condition of affairs making the house unfit for human habitation.'

On 16 July, showery weather presented itself at the annual 'Sing' at the Cawthorne Hospital Festival, on behalf of the Beckett Hospital, and as a result the receipts were considerably affected. There was a capital chorus of 100 voices, led by Mr Butcher. The chairman delivered an impressive speech, making the war and the heroic conduct of our gallant troops his chief topic, and the self-sacrificing labours of the brave and devoted doctors and nurses who were alleviating the sufferings of the wounded.

On 23 July, Sunday was a red-letter day for Darfield. Favoured by exceptionally fine weather, the Annual Musical Festival proved one of the most successful for many years and the committee of the Darfield and Low Valley Hospital Movement organised the whole day's proceedings superbly. At 9.30am a large crowd had already gathered in the Millhouses Recreation Ground, the appointed to watch the morning church parade, amongst whom were Darfield Boy Scouts, members of the Ancient Order of Druids and other Friendly Societies, along with the President, Mr George Scott and members of the committee, headed by the Houghton Main Colliery Band, who proceeded by via Middlewood, Highfield, and School Street (making a collection en-route) to All Saints'

This aerial photograph shows the ground the men of Barnsley were expected to traverse as they attacked the German held village of Serre. The British front line can be seen at the bottom left of the photograph. At 7.20 am on the 1 July 1916, the soldiers of the first wave left their trenches, passed through the British wire and lay down in no man's land to await the end of the bombardment. This ceased at 7.30 am, and in front of Serre men of the 12th York & Lancaster (Sheffield City Battalion) and the 11th East Lancashires (Accrington Pals) who were the first wave stood up and tried to cross no man's land. The attackers were mown down by machine gun fire, although one company of the Accrington Pals did reach Serre, but were lost. Reinforcements, men of the 13th and 14th York & Lancasters (the 1st and 2nd Barnsley Pals) were sent in, but were also stopped with no success, and the attack here was then suspended. Serre remained in German hands.

The Barnsley Chronicle

AND PENISTONE MEXBRO' WATH AND HOYLAND JOURNAL.

VOL. LVIII. NO. 4013   SATURDAY, JULY 15. 1916.   ONE PENNY

Butterfields SALE.

The greatest occasion of the year to save money.

Butterfields
(The Drapers, Ltd.),
1, Church Street,
BARNSLEY.

WONDE

The opportu to buy Dre Licensed, I Increased,

Butterf
(The Drapers
1, Church
BARNSL

LOCAL HEROES FALL IN ACTION.

BARNSLEY BATTALIONS CHARGE THE HUNS

THROUGH SHOT AND SHELL.

OFFICERS & MEN MAKE GREAT SACRIFICES.

Hundreds of troops from Barnsley and district took part in the great British offensive on Saturday, July 1st, in the region of Albert, France, and though they succeeded in carrying out their plans this was done at a great sacrifice of life and limb.

It was about seven o'clock on the morning of the 1st inst. that the order was given for the men of the two Barnsley Battalions, the Territorials, and other regiments to fix bayonets preparatory to leaving their shielded quarters for the move forward. The Germans, it was known, were only about 100 yards away, and no sooner had the Britishers mounted the parapets than they were faced with terrific machine gun and shrapnel fire. Many officers and men were struck down and the casualty list is sorrowful reading.

Grief-stricken parents, relatives, and friends can take consolation from the reading of the observations made by the General leading the Division and which appears in this issue.

FOR KING AND COUNTRY.

PTE. H. ATKINSON (BARNSLEY.)   PTE. J. W. RIDLEY (BARNSLEY.)   PTE. W. TAYLOR (BARNS

PTE. W. FEELEY (BARNSLEY.)   PTE. G. POPPLEWELL (STAIRFOOT)   CPL. A. POPPLEWELL (STAIR

PTE. H. MILLIARD (DODWORTH)   PTE. H. CLARE (CUDWORTH)   LCE.-CPL. T. B. EAMES (WOMB

Church, Darfield's parish church, where a most impressive sermon was delivered by the Reverend A. Thomas, who emphasised the present-day needs of hospitals and our duty as a nation to support them.

The assembly for the afternoon demonstration took place on Low Valley Cricket Field, and long before the hour was fixed the district was simply one vast, animated crowd of men, women and children, all out to do their bit for the sick and wounded.

On Monday, 31 July, at Barnsley Borough Police Court, considerable time was taken up in hearing eight summonses concerning four male employees of the revue company All Aboard, which had played at Barnsley's Empire Palace the previous week. Reginald S. Swift, music hall artiste (and manager), was summoned with contravening section 41A of the Defence of the Realm Regulations and with contravening the Reserve Forces Act 1882. Walter S. Smith, music hall artiste and William G. Forman, comedian, were charged with being absentees from the army reserve and with failing to notify of changes of address and H. Charles Barnaby, stage carpenter, was charged with being an absentee and with failing to produce a certificate of registration when requested to do so.

Lieutenant-Colonel Hewitt said that he appeared in support of the summonses against these defendants. The man Swift was charged under the section of the Reserve Forces Act which stated that anyone who aided any man belonging to the army or reserve who was an absentee without leave, or assisted him in concealing himself, was liable on summary conviction to a fine not exceeding £20. It was well known under the Defence of the Realm Act that this man should have put up a list of the persons in his employ of military age. Swift was the manager of a theatrical revue which had come to the town and the other three defendants were in his employ. During the lengthy proceedings, the chairman was prompted to remark that everybody was supposed to know the law and this applied to the theatrical profession as much as to anyone else.

For failing to exhibit the list Swift was fined 40 shillings (£2). With regard to the other charge, the Bench thought possibly there might have been some difficulty in the matter, but in that case the defendant must have known this man was eligible for the army and he had no right to employ him. For this offence Swift was fined 10s. Smith and Barnaby were fined 5s. each for the registration offences and for being absentees were each fined 40s. and remanded to await an escort. The cases against Forman were adjourned one week to give him an opportunity of

Photographs of casualties and accounts from the wounded filled the pages of the *Barnsley Chronicle*.

producing his birth certificate in support of his claim that he was 41 years-of-age. (On his appearing in court the following Monday the cases against William Albert G. Forman, comedian, were dismissed, having produced a birth certificate showing he was born in 1875 and therefore over 41 years-of-age.)

August 1916

On Saturday, 5 August, the first of what is to be an annual treat for children under the auspices of Worsbrough Common Working Men's Club and Institute, took place in glorious weather. The children paraded through the village headed by the Borough Prize Band, and afterwards children to the number of over 300 were entertained to a sumptuous tea, catered by the Barnsley British Co-operative Society. After tea every child was presented with a suitable toy. During the evening a fine programme of sports was thoroughly enjoyed.

At Cudworth the monthly meeting of the Council met on 9 August. The Medical Officer of Health, Dr J.L. Elliott, reported that during the past month there had been six cases of notifiable disease, namely, two of erysipelas, two of measles, one of pulmonary tuberculosis and one of opthalmia neonatorum. There were fifteen births, and six deaths, giving a birth rate of 25.80 and a death rate of 10.32 (per 1,000 population). The report concluded: 'The health of the township as in the previous month was good.'

> **August 1916 10th**
> The end of the Brusilov Offensive.

Dr Elliott also presented a report with reference to four houses in Sidcup Lane which he had inspected on the instruction of the council. He stated that there were two earth closets to the four houses, and no space at the back to erect two more closets, so he recommended that two water closets be substituted. There were only two coal houses for the four houses and the people preferred to have them locked up and keep the coal in the house.

On Sunday, 13 August, three open air musical festivals were held on behalf of the Beckett Hospital, and each event was attended with much success financially and otherwise. At Gilroyd, a dual effort was made on this occasion, as on Saturday preceding the musical event a horticultural show was held in the morning and sports in the afternoon, on a field kindly lent by Mr H. Allen. Although the attendance was satisfactory, the showery weather kept many people away.

At Grimethorpe, the annual Hospital Festival took place. A procession, headed by the Hemsworth Colliery Band, was formed on the village green at 1.30 pm and paraded the main streets to the Colliery Institute Cricket Field, where hymns and chorus were sung, and selections given by the band. Collections were made en-route and at the gates of the cricket field.

On Sunday evening, the third annual music festival in aid of the Beckett Hospital was held in a field, kindly lent by Mr A. Priest, at Barugh, and 'a fine programme of music' was presented to the appreciative crowd.

On the weekend of the 12 and 13 August, the annual feast took place at Silkstone, where there was a large number of visitors. Various events were organised and well patronised, including cricket matches and military sports. The Silkstone Brass Band paraded and a house-to-house collection was made at Silkstone and Silkstone Common on behalf of Beckett Hospital.

On 23 August, an important case from Stairfoot was placed before the West Riding magistrates at Barnsley, the hearing lasting three hours. George Stenton, landlord of the Keel Inn, Stairfoot, was summoned for allowing 'treating,' contrary to the Liquor Control Board (treating being an offence under DORA: it was illegal to buy drinks for others). His waiter, Stephen Timlin, was summoned for supplying the drinks in question, and other defendants in the case were George Batty, John Thomas Love and Leonard Siddle, all miners residing at Stairfoot; and Tom Moore, miner, from Barnsley. Lieutenant-Colonel Hewitt represented the landlord, the others were represented by Mr Rideal. The incident occurred at about 7.30 pm on Sunday, 13 August, during Stairfoot Feast.

All the defendants, and a number of other men who were in the house denied that any treating took place. The chairman, after the Bench had a brief consultation in private, said they had come to the conclusion that the charges were proved. They quite recognised that this occurred at feast time, when there was considerable difficulty in exercising supervision. On this occasion they took that into consideration, and they hoped that the penalty they were going to inflict would be ample to meet the case, and that there would be no further penalty attached to the charge. He advised the landlord to be very careful in future. They knew the difficulties landlords had, especially on feast occasions and they hoped extra care would be taken. The landlord was fined 40s. on each charge, £4 in all; the waiter £1 on each charge, and the other defendants £1 each.

On Saturday, 26 August, the sixth annual show of the Crane Moor and District Horticultural Society took place, and was attended with great success. Both in quality and quantity the exhibits came up to the usual high standards, which has become expected of this particularly fine society. The standard of excellence reflected much credit on the competitors most of whom were said to be engaged in 'colliery work'. The Society was said to be in a flourishing condition financially, having a bank balance of £25.

September 1916

On Saturday, 2 September, there was a large gathering at a knur and spell match at the Station Inn Grounds, Dodworth, to witness a long-knock match, between Fred Matthewman, of Crane Moor and Wilmot Garnett, of Silkstone, for £25 a side. Matthewman won, the scores being: Matthewman: 9 scores, 10 yards; Garnett, 8 scores, 15 yards.

Milk, which in normal times could be purchased at 4d. a quart, was now being retailed at 6d. a quart. This was a decision arrived at by the Barnsley and District Milk Sellers' Association, at a well-attended meeting presided over by Mr Alfred Swift at the Imperial Hotel. The question of increasing the price of milk for the winter months was discussed at length and the resolution fixing the price at 6d. per quart was carried without dissent. Stress was laid upon the increased cost of feeding stuffs, the scarcity and costliness of labour, and the much larger capital needed to keep the dairy herd going. It was also emphasised that it had been thirteen months since the Association had increased the price to 5d. a quart. It was also resolved by the meeting that on and after the first Monday in October there should only be one delivery of milk per day during the winter, the effect of this being a curtailment of expenses in delivery.

On 13 September, another 'treating' case came before the magistrates at Barnsley West Riding Court, when William Bright, landlord of the Station Inn, Dodworth was summoned 'for selling'; two waiters, 'for supplying'; three customers 'for paying'; and four customers 'for consuming'. The offences occurred on Saturday, 2 September, following a knur and spell match held in the grounds.

The Bench heard that the methods adopted by the police were identical

**September
1916
15th**
The first use of tanks en masse at the Somme.

Four Mark I tanks prepare to go into action at Flers–Courcelette on the Somme, 15 September, 1916.

of those with previous similar cases. Colonel Hewitt, in his address for the defence, said that the landlord had not supplied any intoxicating liquor wrongly, and if he had taken every possible precaution to prevent treating it was absolutely impossible for mortal man to do more. The landlord had taken all possible precautions, and there were seventeen people in the room who would speak as to what took place. The public had every right to be believed as any officers of the law. The police officers were zealous, and went about their duty with a view to finding a case, and whatever might have a semblance of offence would with vivid imagination soon become fact.

It transpired during the landlord's evidence that 230 persons had paid for admission to the knur and spell match and afterwards a number of them came into the public house, causing them to 'become very busy'. The extensive witness evidence stated that all were in a position to see what was going on, and that any 'treating' had taken place was flatly denied. They also said that the landlord several times called out that everyone must pay for his own drink.

The chairman said that the Bench had given every consideration to this case and they found that the charge was proved. Hitherto they had dealt rather leniently with those charged with treating and with being treated, and had come to the conclusion that they would have to impose a more severe fine on these persons. Treating was a severe offence and this provision had been instituted during the period of war. The law would have to be carried out and the treating would have to be stopped. If necessary they would have to increase the fines considerably more. The landlord was fined £5 and the other defendants 30s. each. The chairman then added that the Bench hoped that the fine upon the landlord would be considered adequate for the offence, and that no further penalty would be attached to it by way of suspension of the licence which had been done in some cases.

At the annual meeting of the Wharncliffe Silkstone and District Horticultural Society on the evening of Tuesday, 19 September, 'a very satisfactory report' was presented by the secretary, Mr J.L. Wright. The total income was £81 13s. 4d. and the expenditure, £37 5s. 6d.

The investigation for the Ministry of Munitions by Dr Vernon into the question of industrial fatigue, in relation to the output by women in munition factories in the making of shells had come into special prominence 'under the stress of war conditions'. Dr Vernon's report was said to 'draw a bold distinction between the capacity of men and that of women to endure the strain of concentrated activity,' and suggested that more rest periods should be instituted. Dr Vernon commented: 'This obvious fact is not realised by many managers of munition works, and the tendency is usually towards uniformity of hours for all types of labour, and for workers of both sexes.'

October 1916

On Saturday, 7 October, the quarterly council meeting of the Working Men's Club and Institute Union Ltd was held at Bradford. In the morning the delegates visited several works in the district and in the evening visited various clubs in the city. The South Yorkshire district was represented by Councillor J.H. Bagshaw, of Stairfoot. The principal item of discussion of the report of the executive was an outspoken criticism of the Central (Liquor Traffic) Board. The report asserted that the whole work of the Board was represented by failure. The Board had not diminished the total consumption of drink. It had set up home drinking on an unparalleled scale, it had driven women to familiar acquaintance with public-house bars and independent drinking. It could point to no good result. The events it set up were widespread and if not checked would injuriously affect generations ahead, it was said.

On Tuesday, 10 October, Mr Jonathan Ball (chairman) presided over the meeting of the Barnsley Board of Guardians, when Mr W.J. Hoyland proposed that in accordance with the notice of motion, the amount of relief paid to persons over 70 years of age, should not exceed 4s. 9d. weekly.

The annual galas for testing the children in swimming and life saving were held at Wombwell Baths on the evenings of Monday, 16 to Wednesday, 18 October. The attendance was a record, the accommodation for the building being tested well beyond its capacity. For 1916 there were 560 children on the swimming registers who could swim. Of this number, 432 children gained certificates as follows: life saving: 41; county council: 219; 25-yards certificates: 85; and ten yards: 87. A second examination will be held for those unable to attend the galas, the results of which will considerably increase the above figures.

In addition to other mining districts, Barnsley was well represented on Wednesday, 25 October in London, when the prime minister addressed them on the subject of increased output and absenteeism. At the close of the proceedings a resolution was carried favouring co-operation amongst miners to secure a greater output.

Mr Asquith said the most serious and formidable fact was the progressive decrease since the war began in our output of coal. In 1913 the total output was 287 million tons; in 1914 it fell to 265 million tons; while in 1915 there was a further fall to 253 million tons. The demand was in excess of the supply, and were it not for the Limitation Act we should have seen a large enhance scale of prices here at home. The decrease in output was primarily due to the patriotic action of the miners, who in the early days of the war, recruited in enormous numbers. Up to the end of last June no fewer than 250,000 miners had joined the colours – a magnificent record. A great deal had been done to mitigate the dangers of the situation. Coal owners had stopped all exploratory work and the government had not only stopped recruiting miners, but had returned 11,000 ex-miners. By general agreement the most urgent thing was the reduction of absenteeism. He believed that the vast majority of miners had the utmost detestation for shirking, and he appealed to every man to attend work every day the pit was opened...

Mr Smillie, President of the Miners' Federation, expressed the opinion that the deficiency could be made up by regular attendance at work.

Towards the end of the month, the sanitary inspector to the Penistone District Council reported an outbreak of typhoid fever at High Street, Silkstone, from which two deaths had occurred. There were four cases in one cottage which had been overcrowded, nine persons sleeping in two bedrooms, and an old man slept on the ground floor. The house had been previously condemned as unfit for human habitation, but owing to the war and scarcity of houses the order had not been carried out. A married woman with seven children had nursed the first fever case, that

BARNSLEY PATRIOTIC FUND.

EMERGENCY ACCOUNT as on 4th October, 1915.

RECEIPTS.	£ s. d.	£ s. d.	PAYMENTS.	£ s. d.	£ s. d.
To Donations, including £250 from the National Relief Fund, aad £50 from the "Barnsley Chronicle" Co., Ltd.		311 0 0	By Advances—		
			Grants	485 11 3	
" J. Wildsmith, Donation for Boots		25 0 0	Loans	226 12 0	712 3 3
" Subscriptions from General Fund		932 16 3	" Accounts paid for Boots prior to		
" Bank Interest	0 10 6		formation of Boot Fund	172 4 4	
Less Commission	0 7 0		" Subscriptions to Boot Fund	190 0 0	362 4 4
		0 3 6	" Groceries purchased and distributed		96 3 0
Loans Refunded		89 16 6	" Funeral Expenses of Children		32 5 0
			" Printing, Stationery, &c		19 7 0
			" Petty Cash Items		18 13 4
			" Platform fixing for Concert		5 2 5
			" Collection Boxes		8 9 0
			" Cost of Removal of Families		0 15 0
			" Cheque Books		1 0 0
			" Taxi Hire		2 2 6
			" Balance in Bank as per Pass Book		22 16 2
			" Balance in Hand on Repayment of Loans Account as per contra	89 16 6	
			Less Amounts due to Secretary on Emergency Grants. £9 2 1		
			Sundry Payments ... 2 19 2	12 1 3	
					27 15 3
		£1,308 16 3			£1,308 16 3

J. HEWITT, Chairman.
R. HUGGARD, ⎱ Committee.
FRANK WOOD, ⎰
CHARLES PLUMPTON,
Honorary Secretary.

WM. CARR,
Incorporated Accountant, Barnsley.
18th January, 1916.   Auditor.

of a boy, all the time going backward and forward amongst her own children. A woman slept in the bed from which the boy had been taken a day or two previously, and had contracted the disease and died. It was also stated that soldiers' clothes from the adjoining camp had been washed in this cottage. The council decided that the cottage must be closed at once for human habitation.

November 1916

An amazing story of a daring bank robbery by two schoolboys, aged 10 years and 8 years was told in the West Riding Children's Court, on Monday, 27 November, before Mr W. Duston (in the chair), Alderman J.S. Rose, Mr W.L. Wadsworth, and Mr G.C. Pickering. They were charged with stealing one hundred £1 treasury notes from the Yorkshire Penny Bank at Wombwell (worth £9,276.47 in 2016) on 21 November. It was stated for the prosecution that at this branch of the bank there was only one clerk employed, owing to shortage of staff. About 12.30 on Tuesday afternoon Mr Archer, the manager, was there alone, and he was obliged to leave the front part of the bank for about one and a half minutes. Upon his return he missed a bundle containing a hundred £1 treasury notes. Information was given to the police who found that two boys had been to several shops in Wombwell and purchased, among other things, a white metal 'albert', two watches, and a suit of clothes each, paying for these with £1 notes. They then went firstly to Leeds, then on to Bradford, where they were arrested. The elder boy had in his possession £65 in treasury notes, £3 7s.4d, in cash, a new gent's metal watch, a lady's silver wrist watch, a pocket knife, a new flash lamp and a new foot cycle. The other lad had £13 in treasury notes, 10s, in silver, a new foot cycle, a flash lamp and a packet of cigarettes.

The boys returned by car from Leeds to Bradford, where they were arrested. Between them they had £82 17s. 4d in their possession and Inspector Brimms has since recovered another £4 1s. The elder boy told Inspector Brimms that they both went into the bank, and his companion helped him to get onto the counter. He then took the notes which were laid on another counter and tied up with an elastic band. Each of the lads was ordered to have six strokes with the birch rod.

On Thursday, 30 November, at the Leeds Assizes, before Mr Justice Darling, Elsie Catherine Frost, aged 23, formerly sub-postmistress at Platts Common, pleaded guilty to fraudulently converting £75 1s. 0½d. (worth £7,500 today) to her own use, and to making false entries in

Wombwell Road, Platts Common. Old Barnsley

certain documents while the servant of the Postmaster General. It was stated the prisoner, whose husband was at that time lying seriously wounded in a London hospital, had appropriated over £220 (worth £20,680 today).

Mr C. Mellor, counsel for the prisoner, she did not endeavour to put the blame on anyone else, and she was very sorry for what she had done. Having considered the evidence His Lordship said it was very painful to anyone in the position he was to have to deal with a case like the prisoner's. He said he felt he must protect the State and those who entrusted money to the Post Office. He gave Mrs Frost a sentence of twelve months' imprisonment.

On the same day at Leeds Assizes that Mrs Frost was tried and sentenced, Annie Blyton Turner, a 38-year-old widow, described as a postmistress, also appeared before Mr Justice Darling. She pleaded guilty to charges of embezzling £100 (worth £9276.47 today) on 7 July and £120 (worth £11,131.76) on 5 September, the sums of money taken into her possession in the name of the Postmaster General. Counsel for the prosecution stated that the prisoner was sub-postmistress at Royston, and in July 1916 the Post Office were carrying out transactions on behalf of the government in Exchequer Bonds. A workman deposited £80 and later £20 for the purchase of a £100 Exchequer Bond, but the prisoner did not pay the money over to the authorities. In September a man named Swallow deposited an Exchequer Bond of the value of £120, and the prisoner again failed to report the receipt of the money to the authorities.

Arthur James Watts, of the General Post Office, London, said the prisoner was in receipt of a salary of £138 11s. (worth £12,857.19 today) per annum, and in addition received 28s. (worth £129.87) per week in respect of the work necessitated by the payment of the Army and Navy separation allowances. Out of the latter amount she had to pay an assistant. He understood that the prisoner had two children, and that her late husband, who died in 1913, was the sub-postmaster at Royston, while the prisoner acted as his assistant. Mr Watts added that he believed the prisoner's children had been ill, and she had got into the hands of money lenders.

December 1916
Seasonable weather associated itself with Christmastide in Barnsley and district, but owing to the war, festivities were of a very limited character indeed. The snow-clad streets rendered 'pedestrianism'

somewhat difficult, though despite the weather conditions the influx of visitors was quite up to the average. Consequent upon the curtailed railway facilities, the number of people leaving the town was very limited and this was especially noticeable in the case of long-distance bookings, which were unusually small. It was a great pleasure to many at home to find the military authorities had removed the order to stop Christmas furloughs, and throughout the week many soldiers from the fighting fronts and from camps in various parts of England were to be seen enjoying the festival amongst those near and dear to them. In the weeks leading up to Christmas the General Post Office, had been besieged with senders of parcels to those soldiers and sailors to whom the privilege to come home had not been conceded, and many acknowledgements of consignments of comforts reached their senders. A feature of the Christmas season has been the forwarding of parcels to men at the Front. Messrs Guest Ltd., of Market Hill made a special study of soldiers' comforts and from all parts of the surrounding district found commissions to pack and despatch hundreds of boxes, which were sent through the generosity of various funds. Among these were Penistone Soldiers' and Sailors' Fund (120), Gawber Adult School (19), Woolley Colliery (30) Locomotive Enginemen and Firemen (19), Tankersley Relief (51), Wombwell Main Wesleyans (11), Elsecar Ambulance Class and Earl Fitzwilliam's Colliery (35), Silkstone Choir Fund (48), Woolley Church Comforts Fund (60). The Barnsley parcel with its bright brown wrapper and green strappings was a welcome present 'to our local lads in the trenches'.

At the Beckett, Kendray and Lundwood hospitals, the patients were by no means forgotten, whilst everything possible was done to cheer the inmates of the Union Workhouse. Football devotees were well catered for. A football match at Oakwell on Christmas Day between troops at Silkstone and Redmires attracted a big crowd despite the cold, snowy weather; and substantially benefited the coffers of the Beckett Hospital. On

**December 1916
7th**
David Lloyd George
became British Prime
Minister.

Boxing Day, the Barnsley team entertained Leicester Fosse and gave them a severe beating, thus confirming their previous day's victory on the Leicester soil. At the numerous places of entertainment 'big business' was done.

Owing to the generosity of the townspeople and friends of the Kendray Hospital, the patients and staff had a most enjoyable Christmas Day. The children had well-filled stockings awaiting them in the early morning and later on Father Christmas (Dr Sharpe) distributed presents and articles of warm and useful clothing. At midday, Dr Sharpe officiated at the dinner of patients and maids, which was followed by a gramophone entertainment. The nursing staff had dinner in the evening, and afterwards enjoyed dancing and a whist drive.

The Christmas festivities at the Barnsley Beckett Hospital followed 'the usual lines', the patients having as happy a time as circumstances permitted. The Blucher Street United Methodist Choir sang carols in all the wards on Christmas morning, and the local bands also attended and gave selections of music. Dinner, which consisted of the customary Christmas fare, was heartily partaken of, and each patient received an acceptable present, the children being delighted with well-filled stockings. In the afternoon the patients received their friends. On St Stephen's Day (Boxing Day) the children had a special treat, two Christmas trees being placed in the ward. Mr C. Alderson cut down the presents which were handed round to the little patients by Master Bond and other children. Afterwards the children were entertained by the nursing staff. On 28 December Mr J. Elliott's concert party entertained the patients and on 29 December, Mrs Grocock and party gave an entertainment. The decorations at the hospital during this particular Festive Season were of a simple character but the staff under the direction of Matron, Miss Burkhill, succeeded in making the wards look very pretty. At that time there were seventy-five patients in the hospital, including seven soldiers.

At Lundwood Hospital, where there were twenty-six soldiers convalescing, thanks to the generous response to the appeal in the *Barnsley Chronicle* for contributions the comforts, and 'these brave men had a glorious time'. Dinner on Christmas Day comprised roast turkey, a variety of vegetable and plum pudding, followed by a liberal allowance of cigarettes to each soldier, whilst in accordance with the decision of the Hospital Committee, 'each of the heroes' was supplied with a bottle of beer. The interior of the hospital presented a bright and attractive appearance. In the afternoon a concert party was in attendance and they rendered a most excellent programme of music.

MEETINGS AND ENTERTAINMENTS.

THEATRE ROYAL
AND OPERA HOUSE.
Tuesday, Dec. 26th, and following Four Nights.
No Performance on Christmas Day.

6-50— Twice Nightly. —9-0.

Special Engagement of your Old Favourite,
Mary Austin,
and Popular Company, in an entirely New Play
of Brittany Life—

The Fishermaid of Old
St. Malo.

MARY AUSTIN as "The Fishermaid."

POPULAR PRICES.   25 i1

In accordance with the usual custom, everything possible was done to insure the inmates at the Union Workhouse spent a pleasant Christmas Day. There were in the house that day 184 men, 115 women and 35 children and the day was made 'one of happiness for these poor, unfortunate people'. The walls and corridors were decorated with greenery and Chinese lanterns, creating a very cheerful appearance. Dinner included roast beef, plum puddings, and after full justice had been done to the substantial meal, apples, oranges, sweets and tobacco were distributed. In the evening the staff and inmates were treated to a concert.

During the entire week of the festive season each of the places of entertainment in Barnsley were crowded both at matinees and every evening performance. Lovers of opera were handsomely catered for at the Empire Palace, where the famous O'Mara Company were in evidence. At varying performances they undertook to perform either *Carmen* or *Madame Butterfly*, the final performance on Saturday evening being of *Maritana*. With such a magnificent company that Mr Joseph O'Mara brought to Barnsley, a perfect rendering of all three operas was assured 'much to the delight of the audiences'.

At the Theatre Royal, Miss Mary Austin clearly demonstrated she had lost none of her popularity as an actress as she took the title role in the entirely new drama *The Fishermaid of Old St Malo*, which attracted splendid audiences, the action taking place in Brittany, France. Miss Austin was ably supported 'by a splendid company'.

The crowds assembling nightly at the Pavilion were splendidly entertained by the Famous Sports Company, including singers, dancers, comedians and boxers; where Miss Madge Young, 'the world's cleverest lady boxer', gave ample proof of her claim. The Four Astors, a vocal and dancing act elicited considerable applause.

Topping the bill at the palatial Alhambra was M. Gintaro 'the famous Japanese top spinner and juggler' and other specialities. Kit-O-More and Jim Soho, the one with a 'golden voice' and the other with two eccentric feet, were a distinct attraction, whilst Nevotti, the famous tenor, scored with his chosen repertoire of songs. Susie Marney, chorus

The Olympia Skating Rink opened in 1909 on the corner of Peel Street and York Street. In 1911 it became the Pavilion cinema. Tasker Trust

comedienne, the hoop jugglers Clifford and Grey, Reno, the lady juggler and The Mantons completed a programme 'of first-rate order'.

A 'shocking ice tragedy' took place on Boxing Day afternoon on one of the five ponds at Milton, Hoyland, which resulted in three boys losing their lives. The tragic events unfolded following a number of boys in high spirits, whiling away the holiday, and were greatly taken by the sport of sliding on the ice-covered water. The ice gave way and three of the boys found themselves plunging into the freezing cold pond. They were unable to get themselves out and help not being quickly forthcoming, all three of them drowned. The boys who lost their lives were pit-boy Charles Bishop, aged 15, of 41 Sebastopol Street; pit-boy Granville White, aged 13, of 11 Bethel Street and 11-year-old schoolboy, Charlie Fletcher, of 7 Rock Mount.

The Vicarage (which stood on Park Road) of St Edward's church at the top of Racecommon Road was used as a convalescent home for men who were wounded during the war. Edward George Lancaster of Keresforth Hall had offered the building to the War Office. It opened in November 1914 and treated men with non-life threatening injuries. Dr Sadler was the Lancaster Home's physician and the Matron was Miss Mary Bellamy. The wounded men gave concerts and held sale of work events to raise money for 'health-giving drives' during the spring and summer months, as well as providing for other comforts such as cigarettes and tobacco. Some of the proceeds were donated to the **Barnsley War League.** Old Barnsley

Chapter Five

1917: Climactic Developments

January 1917

Hoyland Common was the scene of great celebrations on New Year's Day. A confetti carnival was held in the miners' institute, where an excellent dance programme was gone through. A successful New Year's gathering was held at the Wesleyan church, where there was a large attendance and an admirable musical programme was contributed by the male members of the church, and guild; and 'the annual New Year's effort' was held at the United Methodist Church, where after supper, Mr J.E. Watkinson presided over an excellent musical programme.

The Barnsley West Riding Court sat for two hours on the morning of Wednesday, 3 January, hearing cases against Albert Royston, landlord of the Barleycorn Inn, Elsecar, charged with permitting drunkenness; and against James Allott, miner, of Elsecar, charged with being drunk on licensed premises. Albert Royston, was further charged with allowing 'treating' contrary to the Liquor Control Order (DORA). Samuel Allott, miner, and Kate Leathers, married woman, were charged with paying, and George Cookson, miner, Margaret Whitworth and Catherine Whitworth, married women, all of Elsecar, all with consuming. All the offences being committed between eight and nine o'clock on Saturday, 9 December last. Lieutenant-Colonel Hewitt defended. On the first charges the Bench were quite satisfied that the cases had been proven. Fortunately there was nothing previously against the landlord, and he was fined £5. Allott was fined 10s. With regard to the charges relating to 'treating', the Bench decided that all the defendants were guilty as charged. Mr T. Norton (chairman) said it was necessary in the interest of the country to prevent excessive drinking and in spite of repeated warnings the landlord had allowed this to go on. He would have to suffer for it and though he was liable to a fine of £100 they would order him to pay £10. Allott and Cookson were fined 40s. each and the three female defendants 20s.

On Monday, 29 January, the Earl of Harewood, Lord-Lieutenant, presided at the quarterly meeting of the West Riding Territorial Association, at York. Colonel W.E. Raley, JP, the representative of the Barnsley County Borough Council, was in attendance. Three co-opted members were needed, two were selected from Barnsley: Councillor A. Chappell, and Sir Thomas Pilkington. In moving the adoption of Councillor Chappell, the chairman said it was in recognition of past services.

The Earl of Scarbrough said the Association which had just gone out of office had been bearing the brunt of the whole of the work of the Territorial Force during the period of the war and he trusted it was not too much to hope that the new Association might see this frightful war through to a conclusion.

The annual report of the Thurlstone Druids Friendly Society showed continued progress. The sick and death fund account showed a credit balance of £2,055 0s. 6d., member's contributions totalled £188 15s. 4d. The amount paid out to sick members totalled £153 15s. 4d.; and in death £72. The society has a membership of 221.

February 1917

On Thursday, 1 February, between fifty and sixty ladies sat down to 'enjoy themselves' at Grimethorpe Ladies' Monthly Patriotic Tea, after which a progressive whist drive was held. The proceeds, £2 14s. were handed over to the Local Fund.

Official notice is given that, in view of the urgent necessity of restricting as far as possible the consumption of all kinds of

> **February 1917**
> **1st**
> Germany's unrestricted submarine campaign began.

The High Street, Grimethorpe

Concert by the 'Lancaster' Byng Boys – soldiers who were convalescing at the former vicarage of St Edward's church. Old Barnsley

petroleum products, it will be necessary in future in stringent compliance with the provisions of Regulation (e) of the Defence of the Realm regulations. Its effect is to prohibit all charabancs or other like vehicles using any kind of motor spirit (which for the purposes of the regulation includes inflammable containing hydro carbons) on excursions or trips, except trips in connection with ambulance or soldiers, or with naval, military or munition workers to or from their work, and also exceptional trips which are certified by the police to be necessary or desirable in the interests of the travelling public.

On the evening of Monday, 19 February, in the Arcadian Hall, Market Street, Barnsley, a number of wounded soldiers under the title of the 'Lancaster Byng Boys', recovering from wounds in the Lancaster Convalescent Home, provided an enjoyable concert, which was patronised by a large and appreciative audience, many persons not being able to gain admittance. The concert, which was in aid of the Soldiers' Driving Fund, had been admirably arranged.

On Wednesday, 28 February, the members of the Barnsley Board of Guardians met at the Union Workhouse, Mr Jonathan Ball, of Royston, presiding. Mr Bray, the workhouse master, said that about twenty-five 'casuals' (tramps) a week passed through the house, of whom only a small portion were able bodied. There were, however, men between eighteen and sixty who pass through the casual ward who might be employed if they could be registered. Men who might be usefully employed should not be travelling up and down the country in this way. It was suggested that national service forms should be obtained and each casual registered and taken in as ordinary inmates and that they should be allowed to stay until work was found for them.

March 1917

At the monthly meeting of Ardsley Urban District Council, on Wednesday, 7 March, the Allotments Committee considered the terms offered for giving up the land required for allotments in Barnsley Road. The terms offered for the land required in Wombwell Road were considered, and applicants for allotments in that location attended. In total at all the locations presently there were ninety-five allotments let and twenty applications in for new plots. In view of recent government initiatives concerning the expansion of allotment provision, the progress being made was proving worthwhile.

At the monthly meeting of Dodworth Urban District Council, on 12 March, the state of public health in the area was cause for some concern. Dr White said that during the past month there had been five deaths and ten births. There had been a rather severe epidemic of measles in consequence of which a school was closed. No fewer than 173 cases had been reported, but the epidemic was now dying out. The number might seem large but in the past there had been just as bad epidemics, though prior to now the cases were not notifiable. A question was asked if the Green Road schools which had been tenanted by soldiers, had been inspected before the children returned to them, it was confirmed that they had not. It was known that there had been some cases of measles among the soldiers. This was regarded as a serious omission and comments were made that the schools should have been thoroughly cleaned. The Education Committee considered that the schools were clean but there had been some unpleasantness amongst local people and certainly no aspersions were being directed at the soldiers, it was now decided that the buildings should be 'stoved' (fumigated) as a precautionary measure.

A large crowd gathered on the George Hotel ground, Low Valley, on Saturday, 17 March, to witness the football match between teams of ladies drawn from the Barnsley National Shell Factory and Sugden's Empire Mills. Mrs Hellawell, of the George Hotel, kicked off and Mr White officiated as referee. It was a very enjoyable match and despite valiant efforts by the ladies of Sugden's Empire Mills, the ladies of the Shell Factory had a 'capital player' in the form of their centre-forward, Mrs Barratt, who scored a hat trick. The result was Shell Factory 5, Empire Mills 0.

A report in the *Barnsley Chronicle* on 29 March concerning Women's National Service, aroused a great deal of interest:

'Women are now being recruited to replace men on the land. Thousands are needed and as they will be doing men's work they must be of good constitution and vigorous. Service on the land is most urgently needed. Terms and conditions were plainly stated by Mr Prothero in his speech at Saturday's [24th] great mass meeting, honoured by the presence of Her Majesty the Queen. The workers needed chiefly: Milkers, Field Workers, Plough Women, Cow Women, Carters and Market Gardeners. And the terms of service are: board and lodging during instruction. One free outfit. Including boots, breeches, two overalls, and hat. Wages: 18s. per week, at least. Forms for offers of service may be had at all Post Offices, National Service Offices and Employment Exchanges.'

April 1917

There was serious concern about the fall in recruitment for the services, especially the army, as can be seen in the following items, reported in the *Barnsley Chronicle*:

NATIONAL SERVICE

THE TASK OF THE NEW DEPARTMENT

Mr Bonar Law told the House of Commons on the 29th that the recruits for the Army since the beginning of this year had fallen

National Service Campaign
(BARNSLEY DIVISION).

A MASS MEETING
Will be held at the
PUBLIC HALL (HARVEY INSTITUTE),
BARNSLEY,
On MONDAY, April 16th, 1917.

SPEAKERS:
Rt. Hon. SIR JOSEPH COMPTON-RICKETT, M.P. (His Majesty's Paymaster General);
SIR JOSEPH WALTON, M.P.,
Supported by
Mr. Councillor BRAY, J. CARRINGTON, Esq., A. CLEGG, Esq., and other influential gentlemen.

Chair to be taken at 7-30 p.m. by His Worship
THE MAYOR.

If you cannot FIGHT for your COUNTRY, ENROL and WORK for it.

short of the number estimated by 100,000. Therefore, there are 100,000 men to be taken from civilian life to fill up the deficit, and the places of these 100,00 must either be left vacant or they must be filled by National Service Volunteers. And Mr Bonar Law has admitted that the Government is waiting to see what is to be expected of the National Service scheme.

Generally speaking, the work of the Agricultural Section of the National Service Department is to supply civilian volunteer labour for agriculture, to meet the demand which will be made by the War Agricultural Committee in each county, acting on behalf of the Board of Agriculture.

MUSCLE AND PLUCK
*We are reaching the climax of the war,
Are you confident that we shall win?*

You have confidence in our Armies and in the leaders of our Armies. You have confidence in the Navy and our famous sailors. From them comes the support for more fighting men. You have no right to rest on your hopes – confidence means nothing without effort. It is for you to release a young and fit man for the front by doing his work.

It is for you to help in piling up munitions, more in building ships, or in cultivating the land. Germany has called upon her civil population; her armies are still powerful and determined to fight to the end; her navy though diminished is still strong. There is a grave danger in over-confidence, in thinking that trouble will not come till it is on you and overwhelming you, and it is too late to do anything. Why should you have confidence that the fighting men can achieve everything, if you have not got the confidence, the spirit, the energy, the determination to do anything? Summon your will-power, be ready with your muscles and pluck. If you want to be conscious of the coming victory, contribute to it. It is only by realising the terrible danger that is facing us that we can realise our inflexible determination to overcome it.

Come forward now!

A form for an offer of service can be obtained at all Post Offices, National Service Offices and Employment Exchanges. Get one and enrol to-day.

Half a million 'Army Substitutes' were also required; and a new

National Service Scheme was introduced, with women as key workers, especially in agriculture:

April 1917
6th
The United States of America declared war on Germany.

16th
France launched an unsuccessful offensive on the West Front.

NATIONAL SERVICE
THE DUTY TO ENROL
500,000 ARMY SUBSTITUTES WANTED

The work of the Women's Land Army, which is enlisting under the terms issued by the National Service Department and the Board of Agriculture, has grown brisk with the improvement in the weather; and the farmers who are training or testing the Volunteers are said to be very satisfied with the results, particularly in all branches of dairy work. 10,000 women are required at once for training for work on the land, 5,000 to be taught milking and dairy work, and 5,000 for general work.

Promising as the start of the National Service Movement has been, the effort for a moment cannot be relaxed if the requirements of the army are to be met. FIVE HUNDRED THOUSAND more men in the Army means FIVE HUNDRED THOUSAND vacancies in essential occupations to be filled either by MEN or by WOMEN. To take one call only for women, it is calculated that there is room for 40,000 on the land in England alone this year. As for the men, the number of Volunteers is far short of what is needed in the trades and industries which we dare not leave depleted. Therefore the word of command is, more urgently than ever, Enrol!

NATIONAL SERVICE
A NEW SCHEME

The War Cabinet have approved a new scheme submitted by the Director General of National Service, after consultation with his Labour Advisory Committee, for supplementing the general appeal for National Service Volunteers.

The special object of the new scheme is to obtain from the less essential industries a sufficient number of suitable substitutes to take the places of men who must be released for military purposes from the more essential industries.

The main feature of the scheme is that it places upon those concerned in the trade itself the responsibility of finding the men with the least possible injury to the trade or hardship to the man.

NATIONAL SERVICE ON THE LAND

'Upon the farmer rests in a large measure the final responsibility

for winning the war.'

The above words, spoken by Mr Houston, Secretary for Agriculture in the United States of America, do not apply to the American farmer, it is hardly necessary to state. Upon the British farmer rests a great and immediate responsibility; and there is abundant evidence that the fact is thoroughly recognised throughout the country. The pressing demand for agricultural workers, both male and female, is being vigorously met by the Agricultural Section of the National Service Department and by the Women's Section of the Department in collaboration with the Board of Agriculture.

APPEAL FOR WOMEN

With regard to women, the National Service appeal for them to enrol in the Women's Land Army is bringing in a steady stream from the very class of strong and healthy young women required. The training of women for farm work is proceeding all over the kingdom, the organisation of the various centres being very thorough, and the housing and welfare of the workers being very carefully attended to. It is hoped to keep these training centres fully supplied with suitable fresh batches of students as earlier batches are placed with the farmers, and also to send direct to the latter those who have experience of farm work.

HOW THE NEW SCHEME WORKS

The issue of an official communiqué last week, notifying the approval by the War Cabinet of a new scheme for supplementing the general appeal for National Service Volunteers, has been followed by a busy time at the National Service Department. Mr Neville Chamberlain's new scheme, which comes into operation on 30th inst. Is to facilitate the procuring of suitable substitutes to take the places of men who must be released for military purposes from the more essential industries, and its leading feature is that the employers and workmen for whom it has been designed will not be required at any stage to make use of the Employment Exchanges.

HOW SUBSTITUTION IS AFFECTED

Demands for substitutes for men called up for military service from trades of primary importance will be received by the Substitution Officer, who will first of all try how far he can meet each demand

Wentworth Castle, Stainborough.

from the National Service Volunteers enrolled in the district. For the rest, he will call upon National Service and Trade communities, and utilise other sources for substitutes at his disposal.

On 26 April, the half-yearly rent audit of the tenantry of Captain B.C.V. Wentworth, of Wentworth Castle, was held at the Strafford Arms Hotel, Stainborough, where an excellent repast was served up in good style by Mr Walter Bedford. Mr J.S. Petch, agent to Captain Wentworth, presided, supported by Mr Alfred Swift (president of the Barnsley Branch of the National Farmers' Union), Mr C.E. Smith (secretary of the Barnsley Farmers' Union) and others. Mr Swift, in proposing the toast of 'Captain Wentworth', observed that this was the sixth audit since the commencement of the war. They had often heard that agriculture was the most important industry in the world and he thought the war had justified that remark and the food problem was a serious one. The government and the country were looking to the farmer and expecting him to do his utmost to produce the maximum amount of food from the land, but the farmer had been handicapped by having, in many instances, his skilled men taken from him. This fact, combined with the bad weather had delayed the sowing of spring corn. Years ago when corn fell in price to such a figure that it did not pay the farmer to grow it, the land was sown with grass. In the years 1841 to 1845 the home-grown supplies of wheat fed nearly 24 million people; today, the wheat home-grown would only suffice to feed 9 million people, the arable cultivation of land having declined to the extent of 4 million acres. It was an unwise policy of the government of any country to be in times of peace indifferent to the industry which supplied the food of the nation and in this respect he knew of no country of any importance

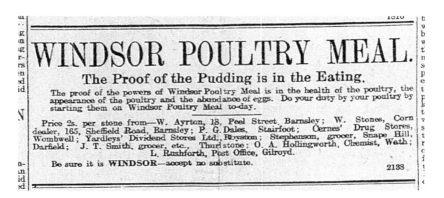

WINDSOR POULTRY MEAL.

The Proof of the Pudding is in the Eating.

The proof of the powers of Windsor Poultry Meal is in the health of the poultry, the appearance of the poultry and the abundance of eggs. Do your duty by your poultry by starting them on Windsor Poultry Meal to-day.

Price 2s. per stone from—W. Ayrton, 18, Peel Street, Barnsley; W. Stones, Corn dealer, 165, Sheffield Road, Barnsley; P. G. Dales, Stairfoot; Cernes' Drug Stores, Wombwell; Yardleys' Dividend Stores Ltd., Royston; Stephenson, grocer, Snape Hill, Darfield; J. T. Smith, grocer, etc., Thurlstone; O. A. Hollingworth, Chemist, Wath; L. Rushforth, Post Office, Gilroyd.

Be sure it is WINDSOR—accept no substitute.

2133

which had so neglected agriculture as had the British government. In his opinion the farmer was somewhat to blame for the apathy he had shown towards unity, and had farmers combined they would have been able to convince the government of the serious food shortage which was likely to occur. The prime minister had declared that never again must the agricultural industry be so neglected and he hoped that that would obtain in the future. In conclusion, Mr Swift maintained that farmers were as patriotic as any other class of people and were ever ready to do their duty.

May 1917

On the evening of Wednesday, 2 May, the annual general meeting of the Barnsley and District Hospital Saturday and Sunday Fund was held in the Town Hall. The income for the year was £259 15s. higher than in any previous year. Including the balance brought forward and bank interest, the total amount collected was £3,258 17s.2d.

On 8 May, during the monthly meeting of the Darton Urban District Council, concerns were again raised about the recent measles epidemic. Dr Millar reported that there had been 5 cases of tuberculosis of the lungs, 117 cases of measles, and 4 cases of German Measles had been notified; and it had been necessary to close the Darton Infant School for a period of five weeks.

Housing was also becoming a serious issue. It was noted that there was a considerable shortage throughout the Barnsley district, especially dwellings that were 'suitable for the working classes'. At the Local Government Board offices on Tuesday, 22 May, Lord Rhondda, president, received a deputation representing practically all national associations interested in the subject of the housing of the working classes. The deputation urged that the government should give encouragement to private enterprise and co-operative effort in the provision of healthy dwellings for the people.

Towards the end of May, in view of the labour shortage in many industries, the appeal for army recruits up to the age of 50 was causing a flutter among employers and also among employees of a class ordinarily considered well beyond the military age. There was no disguising the fact that what made the present appeal so significant was the prevalent opinion that although the enlistment of those veterans was to be a first voluntary, it may prove only the prelude to compulsion.

June 1917

The departmental committee on Juvenile Education after the war issued on Tuesday, 29 May, minutes of the evidence tendered to by witnesses representing both capital and labour, and distributed the same to all parts of the country - and prompted concerns and comments from many local people.

Mr Arthur Balfour advocated a school leaving age of 14 without exemption for poverty or any other reason. The leaving age in Sheffield had lately been reduced to 13 owing to shortage of labour and the urgent need for maintaining of the output of steel, but he felt sure that it would be raised again to 14 as soon as possible. He held that children who took up employment after leaving elementary schools at the age of 14 should attend trade schools in working hours for at least two half-days a week. Attendance should be compulsory, and the employer should be under obligation to allow young people to leave work to attend, and should pay their wages during the time they were attending.

County Alderman W. A. Durnford, JP, of Hoyland, said he was deeply impressed with the need for continuing education beyond the present stage in mining districts, with the object of civilising the pit boys, who as a class, ran practically wild and were entirely undisciplined and too ready to defy their parents, their union and their employers. Very few of them could read or would go to evening schools. In the South Yorkshire coalfield it would not be possible to let them out for two or four hours in the course of a shift for continuation of classes. It would be the lesser of two evils for the boys to be absent for a whole day each week.

In his annual report, the medical officer for Barnsley, Dr P. A. Sharpe, highlighted the acute problems of housing conditions:

'The chief fault lay in building by-laws which had allowed a condition of affairs to arise resulting in a general insanitary state. Chief among these were unpaved common yards, defective means

LEST WE FORGET
THE HONOUR DUE TO
The Heroes of the District
WHO HAVE FALLEN AND THOSE WHO ARE FIGHTING,

should we not each and every one of us send some contribution (even if it must be a small one) for the endowment of the

HEROES' BED
IN THE
Beckett Hospital.

KNOWING AND TRUSTING THE RESIDENTS IN THE LARGE AREA SERVED BY THE BECKETT HOSPITAL THE HONORARY TREASURER APPLIED FOR £1,000 OF WAR LOAN TO ENDOW THE BED AND MAINTAIN IT FREE FOR EVER WITH ITS NAME PLATE AND LIST OF DONORS ATTACHED.

THE STOCK IS BEING PAID FOR BY INSTALMENTS AND ONLY £496 15s 1d. HAS AS YET BEEN RECEIVED. IF YOUR NAME IS NOT IN THE LIST OF CONTRIBUTORS PLEASE SEND A DONATION AND THUS DO YOUR SHARE TO UPHOLD THE HONOUR OF THE DISTRICT AND PERPETUATE THE MEMORY OF THOSE WHO HAVE GIVEN THEIR LIVES FOR YOU.

£503 4s. 11d. IS REQUIRED AT ONCE, AND IT IS BELIEVED THAT THAT SUM WILL NOT BE ASKED FOR IN VAIN.

THE ANNUAL MEETING OF THE GOVERNORS OF THE HOSPITAL IS ON THE 14th OF JUNE, ON WHICH DATE THE PRESIDENT WOULD LIKE TO ANNOUNCE THAT THE WAR STOCK HAD BEEN PAID FOR AND TO PUBLISH A FULL LIST OF CONTRIBUTORS.

of secondary approach, defective cross ventilation of streets, installation of the waste water closet and privy ashpit system, lack of food storage accommodation, and lack of plan in laying out street or fixing numbers of houses to be built on any given area. Even at the present time building lane is being laid out in streets which suits the individual owners' taste and convenience rather than in such a manner that, by the co-operation which a town planning scheme obtains, the needs of the community as to adequate main roads is secured and the number of houses per acre fixed. It had been further established that the sanitary administration was at fault in that proper supervision could not be maintained on account of the fact that a sufficiently numerous staff was not available.'

With regard to back-to-back housing, prevalent throughout the area, Dr Sharpe, made the following observations:

'A back-to-back house is what its name implies, a house having one entrance, the back wall forming the partition it and its fellow. A back-to-back house represents a period in house building when public opinion was unformed and local authorities uninstructed. The cardinal factors rendering these houses undesirable from the sanitary point of view are: (1) They are without means of through ventilation. (2) They are old dilapidated buildings with defective roofs, walls, spouting, plaster, doors, stairs, windows, chimney, fireplaces and floors. (3) Those fronting on a street, for instance Pall Mall, or New Street, are without direct access to a yard and its sanitary convenience, they are supposed to use the yard in common with the houses which, fronting on the yard are back-to-back with them. (4) On account of the low rent those houses command, and possibly their proximity to the centre of the town, a class of tenant is attracted in which the desire

A courtyard in Baker Street which was just off New Street, showing the conditions many were living in. Although this photograph was taken c1930 it would have changed very little from the First World War era.

for sanitary amenities and the ability to ensure them is frequently absent.'

Dr Sharpe continued:

'In my opinion all back-to-back housing is unfit for human habitation, on the grounds stated above. It is true that particular objections can be removed, for instance by making two back-to-back houses of two rooms each into a through room house containing four rooms. Similarly, the condition of the roofs, walls and floors can be remedied. Indeed, in some cases during past years alterations of this kind have been carried out with satisfactory results.'

July 1917

As the war escalated and more demands were made of the British public to put every possible effort into their efforts to ensure victory, hopes for a better future were on many people's minds.

Barnsley it is hoped will participate in at least some of the new and novel industries which are expected to boom after the war. What these are Dr Addison as Minister of Munitions vividly outlined in the course of his recent speech descriptive of the wonderful achievements accomplished in many of the munition shops and factories of this country working under war conditions. As a number of trades and manufacturers in these parts are dependent on the steel industry, as it is important to not that there has been a great increase in the output of this material. The arrangements to increase the use of home ores involve extensive modification of our blast and steel furnaces. By a scheme now in operation it is hoped by next may there will have been added to the country's production of basic steel from home ores nearly two million tons. In various other directions important new industries are being developed. Germany is obtaining all her nitrates without a single cargo coming from Chile. Possibly a key to the solution of this mystery may be found in the statement that there is now to be established in the North of England works for the production of nitric acid from the air! The process is stated to be an extremely simple one, consisting as it does in causing a current of air to pass through the flames of an electric arc, in the heat of which oxygen and nitrogen combine, forming nitric oxide. It is pointed out that the immense demand for nitric acid preparation of explosives, but also for the manufacture of fertilisers and other products, makes this development one of special importance. Nor in the words of the minister of munitions, can Germany any longer hold us to ransom, as formerly for potash. Mr Kenneth Chance has discovered a process for securing all the potash needed for the glass trade and nearly all required for agriculture. In fact, according to Dr Addison, a whole group of industries concerned with the glass trade have been placed on a secure foundation.

As in many other districts in Barnsley, the importance of the cultivation of fruit and vegetable by the ordinary citizens became increasingly important. The fact the many householders, some with families, had little if any garden space available at home to cultivate, highlighted the importance of developing suitable land for this hugely beneficial asset to the local population. The protection afforded to allotment holders by

DORA, served to emphasise the importance the Government laid on the development and maintenance of allotment schemes nationwide. At the monthly meeting of Worsbrough Urban District Council in July, Mr Smith, chairman of the allotment committee, said that all the allotments were progressing satisfactorily. The gateways were not finished, and the committee suggested the erection of notice boards warning trespassers. It was decided to erect these boards. The surveyor, Mr Whittaker, said that he had not received the material ordered from the Board of Agriculture for the potato sprayer, and last week he had reported to him from several sources that an epidemic had attacked several lots of potatoes. He had purchased a potato sprayer, as instructed, and also a small supply of chemicals. Spraying had commenced that day with what materials they had.

The chairman reported on the visit to Birdwell of the government's inspector in regard to the Birdwell Allotments Limited's application for land, and said that the inspector astonished them by stating that all that they had to do was to take possession of the land, and immediately let it to the allotment holders. They had simply to exhibit a notice to that effect, and the trick was done. Mr Penlington added that the inspector then proceeded to tell them that it would be as well if the occupiers of the land and the would be allotment holders could come to terms. Mr Smith said the committee had since met and the prospective holders were willing to stand the cost of acquiring the land. Two sites were under negotiation: an acre of land behind Wentworth Street, in the occupation of Mrs Sausby, and half an acre behind Sheffield Road, belonging to Mr G.F. Smith.

Though showers interfered with the annual music festival at Cawthorne, held in Cannon Hall Park, in aid of the Beckett Hospital, the event proved as popular as ever. On the previous afternoon the soldiers from Silkstone camp provided an excellent programme of sports which were well-attended.

The Barnsley Feast Carnival had a most encouraging send-off when a concert on its behalf was given in the Barnsley Empire Palace, being a great success from both the entertainment and box office points of view. This happy result was in no small part assured by the news that Miss Florence Smithson, the talented and versatile artiste from the music halls and for several seasons past the principal girl in the Drury Lane pantomime, had kindly consented to break her journey from Newcastle to Manchester and make an appearance. As on former occasions when Miss Smithson has graced the Empire Palace stage, 'in the sweet cause

The Empire Palace on Eldon Street was opened in 1908. It was gutted by fire in 1954. Tasker Trust

July 1917
31st
The start of the third
Battle of Ypres.

of charity', she came before the footlight, to enchant an audience crowded in every part of the building. Individually, the other artistes on the bill acquitted themselves in a manner worthy of the occasion. The success of the concert was due to the enthusiastic work of the entertainments committee.

August 1917

As news from the battlefront continued to spur on the efforts of those at home, some concerns were being raised about the time it was taking to bring these hostilities to an end; and at what cost notwithstanding the horrendous loss of life of so many of Britain's youngest and fittest men.

King Louis XIV, once speaking of the power of gold as a resource and staying power in war, said: 'It's the last sovereign that wins.' But in the war that is now raging at present we all know now that man-power and munitions count as well as money-power. Nevertheless, money is a potent factor in war as well as in peace. That is why Parliament has been lately giving anxious consideration to this country's expenditure on the war. The truth is that neither Parliament nor the nation has yet quite overcome the surprise occasioned by Mr Bonar Law's recent statement that the country's outlay has bounded up to eight million a day – £330,000 an hour! It is evidently time that Parliament, which is supposed to exercise certain constitutional checks on the national expenditure, gave attention to this important matter. Before the war this nation's public debt was £650 million. Now it has reached the colossal figure of nearly four thousand million pounds, and it is increasing at a rate of £182 million a month. The question may well be asked, what becomes of all this money? A considerable portion of it is borrowed. Consequently, so long as people are willing and able to lend, and the national credit remains good, the war, so far at least as this county is concerned, is not likely to stop on account of want of funds.

In the grounds of Beckett Hospital, in the presence of a large gathering, Miss Fountain, of Birthwaite Hall, presented a motor ambulance to the committee of the Hospital Saturday and Sunday Fund. Miss

The Beckett Hospital.

Fountain's generous gift supplied a long-felt want in the town and is much appreciated by the residents in the district served by the hospital. The ambulance, which was inspected by the visitors and much admired, is a smooth-running Studebaker, fitted with four stretchers, which are collapsible, and of a very useful type.

19 July: unprecedented scenes were witnessed at the Shaw Lane Cricket Ground, where the athletic sports in connection with the carnival were held under delightful conditions. An enormous crowd assembled and the weather happily turned out to be ideal for the function. In front of the pavilion was fixed a large platform on which a massed orchestra of which some fifty musicians, together with the Barnsley Male Voice Choir were accommodated, and the concert was greatly enjoyed by the magnificent concourse of people in attendance.

Barnsley Feast week was a glorious harvest time for the proprietors of the various places of entertainment in the town. At the Theatre Royal, Mr Vivian Edmonds once again showed his versatility as an actor in his latest success, *A Sailor's Wedding Ring*. Crowded audiences have assembled twice nightly.

The utmost difficulty was experienced in obtaining a seat at the Pavilion, where Mr Harold Feber, the 'Secret Service Man', proved to be a big attraction. Across the way at the Princess Picture Palace, where films of the very best have been consistently displayed, the attractions for the Feast were stupendous. During the week at the Empire Palace the original Eight Jutland Boys were the main attraction.

September 1917

On 4 September, considerable dissatisfaction was expressed in the Yorkshire Coal Exchange in Leeds at the action of the Coal Controller in commandeering supplies in Yorkshire house coal for London, irrespective of local requirements. Serious dislocation is being caused in the distributing of trade throughout Yorkshire and Lancashire as a result of London receiving priority in supplies.

The same day, a special meeting of the Barnsley County Borough Council was held in the evening. The minutes of a meeting of the Health Committee were submitted. Regarding the Pindar Oaks Estate, the Committee recommended the confirmation of the arrangements made by the chairman in taking over the greenhouses and certain of the fixtures in the house, at a cost of £25. The chairman submitted a communication from the secretary of the Eccentric Club's Hostel, asking to be allowed the use of the house at Pindar Oaks, rent free, as accommodation for disabled soldiers under a scheme in which the club accepted full responsibility for its maintenance. The committee unanimously resolved to recommend the council to grant the request, the tenancy to be terminable by one month's notice.

On 5 September, 'gloriously fine weather' favoured the carnival jumble sale held on Wednesday in the cattle market, where the sale of articles of every conceivable description took place. After several other gifts have been disposed of, and various outstanding subscriptions gathered in, it is computed that the Barnsley Charities Carnival will realise the very satisfactory sum of £250.

On 10 September, at Monday's evening meeting of Worsbrough Urban District Council, the circular inquiry of the Local Government Board, relative to the housing of the working classes took place. Mr Steele reported that the committee met and completed the required form and they asked the surveyor to prepare forthwith a scheme. They suggested that fifty houses should be built immediately and hinted that they might probably ask for a hundred.

THE BARNSLEY BRITISH

CO-OPERATIVE SOCIETY

(Limited).

YOU WANT SOME SUGAR DON'T YOU?

THEN REGISTER YOUR NAME NOW.

In connection with the Food Control Scheme, it is highly important that

All Co-operators should Register

their Names at the Branch Grocery Store at which they trade. They will then secure

SUPPLIES OF SUGAR (and other goods which may be "controlled") equal to what could be obtained elsewhere.

THEY, AS CO-OPERATORS,

will PARTICIPATE IN THE PROFITS that remain, when the cost of product and expenses are deducted.

Those desirous of becoming Members of the Society may join at the Central Offices or any Branch Store on payment of 2/6, 1/- of which is entered in the Share Book.

THERE IS NO PROFITEERING.

All PROFITS, after payment of expenses,

ARE DIVIDED AMONGST THE MEMBERS.

In the *Barnsley Chronicle* on 15 September, an article appeared concerning a decision made at a special meeting of the borough council only two weeks before, which must have given great satisfaction to the members of the council:

'The opening of a hostel in Barnsley this week by G. N. Barnes, the well-known Labour minister, is an event thoroughly in accord with local sentiment, the new institution being specially intended for the gallant men who have been sorely stricken in the fierce fight for England's honour and freedom. Nowhere is there truer or more sterling sympathy with these heroes than in Barnsley. That is why the Town Council, promptly and faithfully interpreting local patriotism, has facilitated in every possible way the acquisition of the hostel. When the Council was approached on the subject it at

once agreed to allow rent free the use of the house at Pindar Oaks for the purpose of the hostel. The scheme is being worked by the Eccentric Club who have already established six of these admirable institutions where our disabled warriors, after being supplied with artificial limbs, are given skilled instruction in various occupations so as to enable them to earn their own living. It is a grand work and undoubtedly deserves all the public support it can obtain. Obviously the aftercare of our discharged soldiers and sailors is a splendidly patriotic work, and the training of these heroes for skilled trades is welcomed by the men themselves, opening out as it does to them the bright prospect of augmenting their pensions and augmenting an honourable living. Indeed, the work is so important that it ought to be undertaken by the Government itself. Pending that time, however, such a scheme as has been inaugurated in Barnsley this week merits every possible praise and assistance. Certainly in the light of Barnsley's noble record in this matter it can assuredly be averred that our people are not lacking in their practical recognition of this special obligation, for Barnsley patriotism and generosity are just proverbial.'

On 15 September, in the *Barnsley Chronicle*, was the following:

'From the Town Clerk of Barnsley we have received a copy of a letter sent to the Barnsley Corporation from the Canal Control Committee advising the larger use of the canal system at the present time with a view to minimising the traffic on the railways. The letter was referred to at the County Borough Council meeting (reported in this newspaper last week) and the hope expressed by Alderman W. E. Raley that Barnsley traders would take advantage of the canals and so relieve the pressure on the railways.'

On 29 September, the *Barnsley Chronicle* reported:

'There is much that is wrong in the life-and-death struggle for national existence in which we are engaged. War is a satanic germ: it is a crime against humanity and civilisation; but in this present war we are bound together in one common cause – eg., to defeat militarism either in Germany or elsewhere. And when all is over, it is hoped that out of the debris will spring up greater nations and peoples ready to meet the new and changing conditions, which the world is bound to suffer from, until it regains its equilibrium from the Emperor who has shaken it.

Woman's work has been revolutionised, and almost in every industry at the present time there is a woman in it. We often heard in pre-war days of the toils of our womanhood at the top of the pits and making chains in the Midlands, but few anticipated the day when women would become a very important factor in our engineering and munition factories. Here they are face to face daily with danger, working, not weeping – many for their husbands just across the narrow neck of water near Dover, many awaiting the day when Peace with Honour shall be declared.'

October 1917

The demands of the nation today on its people are enormous – it requires no shirkers; and in many an engineering workshop may be found the woman riveting by machinery, working and turning at the lathes, and in some cases forging at the forge. In many of their hearts there are silent sorrows. There may be the loss of a husband or a son on the gory fields of France, but she plods along with tools and machines, and in her work she forgets 'self' and sees a great whole whose very existence depends on the output of materials for the destruction of both life and property, and amidst the fallen and falling her other sisters are attending to the agonies of the battlefield. Could anything be more paradoxical from a woman's standpoint, than seeking to help make materials to destroy and at the same time with the self-same hands tending the destroyed?

On 14 October, the Sunday-night concert given at the Theatre Royal in aid of the Barnsley Charities Carnival, gave 'unalloyed pleasure to a crowded and appreciative audience', who clearly immensely enjoyed the popular local soprano, Madame Amy Joyner, who was making her first concert appearance following her recent return from the war zone.

'**Barnsley Chronicle' Tobacco Fund.**

FOR ALL SOLDIERS.

Ordinary Cost, **9/10** | Parcel and Postage for **3/3** | Special by Coupon.

CONTENTS OF PARCEL:—

½-lb. United Service Tobacco, usually sold at 8d. per oz.; 200 Cigarettes (Woodbines); Carriage 1/-. Or—

Z. —280 Wills' Woodbine Cigarettes 3/3
X. —575 Ditto Ditto
W.—3 pounds Wills' United Service Mixture 5/7
V.—280 Wills' Gold Flake Cigarettes 5/6

A POSTCARD ALREADY ADDRESSED BACK TO YOU FOR YOUR FRIEND'S ACKNOWLEDGMENT IS ENCLOSED IN EVERY PARCEL.

PARTICULARS OF PARCELS MAY BE OBTAINED AT THE "CHRONICLE" OFFICE, OR MR. ELSTONE, TOB ACCONIST, MARKET HILL.

"**CHRONICLE**" **TOBACCO FUND.**

I enclose 3/3 for one parcel of Tobacco, to be sent to

Regt. number .... Rank ....
Name ....
Squadron, Battery, or Company } ....
Battalion........... Regiment..................................
H.M. Ship ....
Name of sender ....
Address ....

OVER 6,500 PARCELS ALREADY SENT.

Miss Lily Smith, contralto, also of Barnsley, and the well–known baritone, Mr John Browning, also entertained. The Theatre Royal Orchestra under the direction of Mr A. Benson, in the selection 'Morning, Noon and Night', gave an enjoyable contribution.

On 22 October: a meeting of the council of the Yorkshire Miners' Association was held at Barnsley. The president, Herbert Smith was in the chair. At the end of the agenda, votes of sympathy were passed with the relatives of 105 members who had lost their lives, the Association's losses to date being 3,115.

On 29 October: this Monday evening the principal item on the agenda at the quarterly meeting of the Barnsley Chamber of Trade was the question of Christmas holidays. It was recommended to the general body of Barnsley traders to close on Christmas Day (Tuesday) and also on Wednesday and Thursday. It was suggested that this arrangement might not suit grocers, and it was agreed in their case they would slightly deviate from the proposal. The meeting also agreed that shops should keep open the whole day on the Thursday before Christmas (Thursday being half-day closing in Barnsley town). It was also agreed to apply to the Home Secretary through the National Chamber of Trade, for an extension of trading hours on Christmas Eve.

> October 1917
> 24th
> The Battle of Caporetto – the Italian army was heavily defeated.

November 1917

Woman's labour in engineering at the present time is 'a war-time emergency problem' and whether it has come to stay or not will be for the future to stay. It must be 'a strong physical womanhood' which will bear the wear and tear in many works; it has to be an efficient one to make khaki in the factory; and many a noble heart has failed under the strain which the present times are demanding.

Enormous strides have been made during wartime to better the conditions of the workers, especially under government control, by means of welfare and other institutions, and certainly many of the workshops are approaching the ideal from a health standpoint, but these avail nothing if the physical forms are unfit.

On 3 November: on a wet and miserable Saturday a fair crowd watched a match at Oakwell between the Royal Engineers, stationed at Silkstone, and the staff of the Barnsley Recruiting Office. The weather was inclement and the ground heavy. In the first half the Engineers had much the better of the game, the score at half-time being 3-0 in their favour. In the second half the recruiting staff played better, but did not score and the engineers won 9-0. The proceeds were for the wounded soldiers and yielded about £20.

> **November 1917**
> **6th**
> The British launched a major offensive on the Western Front.
>
> **20th**
> British tanks won a victory at Cambria.

On Sunday, 11 November, the Barnsley public were afforded a unique spectacle in the form of an ambulance train constructed by the Lancashire and Yorkshire Railway Company, to the order of the War Office, for use on the continent. The 'magnificent hospital on wheels' was brought to the Lancaster and Yorkshire Railway station before noon and from that time a perfect stream of residents formed a queue extending from the station platform right along Eldon Street for several hours. A charge of 1s. each was made and the proceeds (together with that raised from the sale of small Union Jack flags and book souvenirs) were handed to the fund for providing comforts for British and American soldiers and sailors.

The following notice about 'food control' appeared in the *Barnsley Chronicle*, under the heading: HOW THE MASSES WILL BE FED :

> *The Food Controller and the Director of Food Economy have repeatedly urged upon local committees the importance of being prepared with the necessary arrangements for feeding masses of the people should there be any serious or sudden breakdown of food supplies. Central kitchens are to be established only for the preparation and supply of cooked food to be consumed off the premises, but it will sometimes be advisable where there is a large populous area to be served, to arrange in addition for a number of distributing depots. Kitchens are to be self-supporting so far as possible. They shall be free from the element of charity, and so conducted that any person may use them with self-respect. Grants will be made by the Ministry of Food towards the initial cost of equipment, and orders will shortly be issued dealing with the financial of the question and legalising the establishment of central kitchens by local authorities or other persons acting on their behalf.'*

December 1917

The role of women during the war continued to attract interest:

'Engineering for women is comparatively a new sphere of labour and much of it is of a mechanical description, but it has a fascination about it which appeals to the gentler sex, and she is, as a rule, happy amongst it. There are whispers that on the demobilisation of the Army we may be faced with a greater problem in the world with the women than even the suffrage movement and this is, she will have found the work of such sufficient interest that she will want to keep her position in the industry.

This may occur in some cases, but there is the nobler part of womanhood – that which inspired her to assist in work of high national importance; that which will inspire her in the years to come to lay down tools for her stronger sex and for her to take her rightful place in the homes of the nation's workers. And when the pages of history come to be writ of the Great War there will have to be chapters devoted to the womanhood of the country, who, at a time of great national peril, nobly assisted in the engineering and munition works all over the land.'

On 4 December: addressing a deputation of women in London on Tuesday, Lord Rhondda made some pointed observations on the food question. Several speakers made a point of the hardship involved to women standing in queues outside shops during inclement weather, and urgent in some places that feeling was becoming very bitter. Mrs White (Glasgow) produced sweets, shortbread, and cakes in proof of the contention that essentials were being used for the manufacture of luxuries.

Lord Rhondda, in his reply, said there was nothing very fresh in what had been said. It did not rest with him to decide finally whether there should be compulsory rationing or not; he would represent their view in the proper quarter. He added, 'If and when compulsory rationing comes – I won't say if or when – but if it is put into force, rely upon it, it will be on a reduced scale compared with Sir Arthur Yapp's voluntary scheme. Sir Arthur Yapp's schedule is over forty or fifty per cent higher in food values than the compulsory rationing scheme in force in Germany.'

On 4 December: at the monthly meeting of the Royston Urban District Council on Tuesday evening, housing was the principal subject of discussion. The council were told they had been invited to send representatives to a conference on housing and town planning after the war to be held at Sheffield for three days, from Wednesday, 12 December. Mr Griffiths said the members of the council were working men and the costs involved, even with expenses could not be justified The council decided not to attend, some members protesting that they would get nothing if they did. However, it was clear that when the war was over the three things on which they would have to concentrate were, housing, education and reconstruction. Mr Griffiths said he did not know which was the most important, but in a mining community such as theirs housing was the most burning question, because there was a large amount of evils around it. The chairman said that suitable land for a housing scheme had been offered by Sir Theodore Brinckman at a very reasonable price and after further discussion the clerk said the council would have to prepare a scheme to obtain sanction from the Local Government Board.

> **December 1917**
> **5th**
> Armistice between Germany and Russia was signed.
>
> **9th**
> Britain captured Jerusalem from the Turks.

A joint housing conference of the Urban District Councils of Bolton-upon-Dearne, Darfield, Rawmarsh, Swinton, Wombwell, Wath-upon-Dearne and the rural districts of Rotherham, was held at the Town Hall, Wath-upon Dearne. Councillor John Hinchcliff, Wath-upon-Dearne, presided, and a report was presented by the executive committee. This, with a few slight alterations, was adopted unanimously. The decision arrived at was that there exists urgent need for further housing accommodation in the districts represented.

To meet such need it is estimated that the number of houses required in each of the districts was as follows: Bolton 801, Darfield 200, Mexborough 200, Swinton 200, Thurnscoe 200, Wath 500, Wombwell 700 (with regard to Bolton a scheme for 301 houses has already been passed). Also, that the government be respectfully urged to lend money to the local authorities concerned for the erection of of 2,579 houses proposed to be built by them, on as favourable terms as possible, both as regards the periods of repayments and the rate of interest to be charged. And the Local Government Board will be asked to permit local authorities to rescind or amend any building by-laws which hamper building operations within their several areas without securing any sanitary advantage. Local Government Board also to be asked to frame a new set of model building by-laws for the guidance of local authorities.

Reports received by the Ministry of Food show that Food Control committees in all parts of the country are considering how to abolish the 'evil of queues' and are engaging schemes for that purpose. Lord Rhondda accordingly has made an order giving Local Food Control committees power to control supplies of margarine within the areas for which they are responsible and make arrangements for the equitable distribution of such supplies between the various provision shops of the district.

At the annual meeting of the Yorkshire Miners' Association at Barnsley, held just before the break to indulge in the delights of the Festive Season, the question of food queues was discussed, and the council passed a drastic resolution asking the government to at once step into the breach and remove the anomaly of some people having food sent to their homes and others having to wait in queues for hours. They considered that the time was right for rationing and letting everyone have an equal share of available supplies. The president, Herbert Smith, said that taking into consideration the arduous work some men had to do, the council meeting was determined that unless something was done speedily, instead of women and children standing in queues, it would be the duty of the workman to demand his fair share before doing any work. The present state of affairs, added Mr Smith, was a disgrace to the country.

Christmas Day in Barnsley and district was one of the finest in the matter of weather that could have been wished for. Although biting cold, there was a clear sky and a bracing breeze, which induced many to venture out of doors before noon. One commentator observed that:

'Some folk must have taken some appetites quite capable of doing justice to whatever might have been their fortune to have on the table this war-time. Barnsley and district has seen quite a big number of their Khaki-clad sons over on leave for Yuletide, and one may have read of some area being swarmed with soldiers enjoying a respite from the battle zone.'

At the various hospitals and public institutions the patients and inmates have, as usual been well cared for. At Lundwood and Beckett hospitals, as well as the Lancaster Convalescent Home, Mount Vernon Sanitorium and the Union Workhouse, the interiors were made as cheerful as human hands could make them, whilst the fare provided was on all hands admittedly good.

The railway stations were certainly busy, but the amount of traffic was not to be compared with what occurs in normal times. At the General Post Office the augmented staff easily got through their task. It was noticeable that this year the number of greeting cards was considerably less than in recent years. From day to day the streets of Barnsley were thronged with people, despite the fact that the shopkeepers had decided to close for three successive days from Tuesday (Christmas Day itself, until Friday, 29 December). At Oakwell on Boxing Day a fair-sized home crowd saw their team vanquished by their neighbours Rotherham.

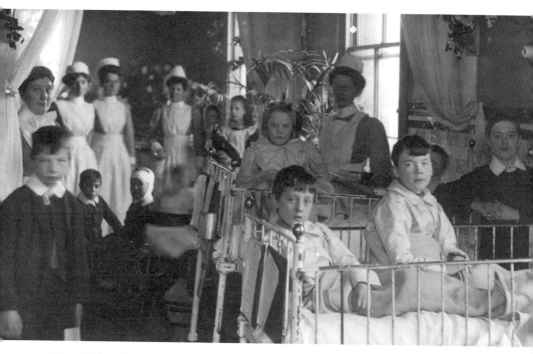

The children's ward at Beckett Hospital decorated for Christmas.

At the Beckett Hospital the various wards were beautifully decorated with evergreens. And everything possible was done to brighten the lives of patients who numbered about ninety, including half-a-dozen soldiers. On Christmas Day the dinner was as sumptuous as ever. Following this most appreciated festive feast, relatives and friends of the patients were admitted and during the day several parties of vocalists gave acceptable 'turns', whilst the Salvation Army Band discoursed appropriate music both outside and inside the institution.

On Boxing Day, Mr Scholey's Pierrot party were in attendance and on 28 December the child patients had their annual treat, when two Christmas trees heavily laden with presents, for each child. The elder patients had presents too, these being even more numerous than during normal times. On Christmas Day evening the nursing staff had their annual dinner and on the following evening the maids had enjoyed a similar feast. Thanks to the energies of the staff under the superintendence of Mr J.W. Webster (master) the various wards were tastefully adorned. On the evening of Christmas Day an excellent concert was given by Mr Scholey's party.

The matron of Lundwood Military Hospital expressed a desire to

TO ENSURE HAVING YOUR USUAL
Christmas Turkey, Goose, Duck, Fowl,
Pheasant, Hare, or Rabbit,
PLACE YOUR ORDERS EARLY WITH
JAMES JUBB,
POULTERER AND GAME DEALER,
CHURCH STREET.
Telephone No. 50.

A view of Church Street in the 1920s. James Jubb's shop is seen on the left of the photograph (circled) where Regent Street meets Church Street. Tasker Trust

thank all those who had helped to make the 'Tommies' such an enjoyable Christmas. Similarly, the matron and wounded soldiers at the Lancaster Convalescent Home offered their very grateful thanks to their friends who had helped to make their Christmas so happy. Also during Christmastide the patients at the Mount Vernon Sanatorium had a really happy and enjoyable time.

The Christmas menu at the Union Workhouse comprised roast beef, plum pudding, cake and fruit and to those good things the inmates did ample justice. Extras in the form of tobacco for the men and sweets for the women were also provided, whilst the children had presents of toys and sweets.

Chapter Six

1918: The End Game

January 1918

During the first week of January every mail delivery brought its quota of letters to the Mayor of Barnsley (Alderman Henry Holden) from every part of the war zone as well as from training quarters in England, thanking his worship for the 'splendid parcels of comforts' which were despatched in readiness for Christmastide. Some of the effusive letters that were received, which could be counted in their hundreds, bore testimony of the thankfulness which the recipients had felt in getting such a happy and practical reminder of the old town.

THE ALHAMBRA, BARNSLEY.

First Performance 6-55—Twice Nightly—Second Performance 9-0.

MONDAY, January 7th, 1918, and during the Week.

E. C. JAZON and M. MONTGOMERY present their GORGEOUS COMIC

PANTOMIME,

The Babes in the Wood

Written, arranged and produced by E. C. JAZON.

GRAND SNOW BALLET

Augmented Orchestra & Chorus under the direction of C. C. Corrie.

Specialities by the Bing Girls, Zoe, Vi & Mac, Laurie and Elsie Quartette.

Boxes 10/6, Tax extra; Orchestra Stalls 1/1, Tax extra 4d.; Dress Circle 1/-, Tax extra 3d.; Upper Circle 9d., Tax extra 3d.; Pit 6d., Tax extra 2d.; Gallery 3d., Tax extra 1d.

Jan. 14th, Miss MARY LAW, the celebrated English Violinist.

On Monday, 7 January, at the Barnsley West Riding Police Court, before Mr G.H. Norton (in the chair), Mr W. Duston, Mr G.C. Pickering and Mr J. Waites - the well-known boxer, Charles Hardcastle, of Worsbrough Bridge - was summoned by his wife, Mabel Hardcastle, for persistent cruelty. When the case was called up, Mr Rideal, for the defendant, said he had some conversation with Colonel Raley (who represented the complainant), and he intimated his willingness to consent to an order of one guinea per week for the present. Colonel Raley said he was prepared to accept that offer, subject to the approval of the Bench. The chairman said the amount was not much, and the Bench thought it ought to be 25s. When asked for her opinion, the complainant said 21s. (one guinea) was not so much. Mr Rideal said it was hoped that

Boxer, Charles Hardcastle.

the couple would get together in a home of their own. They had been living with the defendant's parents. He added that the defendant was a ropeman; to which Colonel Raley added: 'And a champion boxer.'

Mr Rideal then commented that 'Boxing is a very precarious living,' a comment to which Colonel Raley swiftly replied, 'Not if you win.' After some deliberation the Bench made an order of 21s. per week.

The outstanding feature of the proceedings at the monthly meeting of Monk Bretton Urban District Council, chaired by Mr J.W. Shaw JP, was the gratifying announcement that in the township the number of allotment holders had reached 400, this being singled out as a fine example to other districts within Barnsley.

The *Barnsley Chronicle* took the opportunity on the announcement of these encouraging figures to remind those who might have the urge to trespass on allotments exactly what penalties they could incur as the result of such an act:

> '*In order to protect the cultivators of odd pieces of land in the urban districts the Regulation under the Defence of the Realm which was made last spring provided that any person trespassing or doing damage on any plot taken for an allotment or field garden under the Regulation should be guilty of any offence against the same. Allotment holders were advised to post notices on their plots stating that "this land is an allotment or field garden on which crops were being grown, and any person who without lawful authority remains on the land or damages any growing crops or fence or hedge thereon, will be guilty of a summary offence against the Defence of the Realm Regulations and upon conviction will be liable to a fine of £100 (worth £9,246.47 in 2016) with or without imprisonment"*'.

Friday, 25 January: the justices sitting at Barnsley West Riding Police Court were occupied for a length of time in investigating a large number of robberies from the Midland and Great Central Railway Company's premises at Royston and Carlton, and at three local collieries. The prisoners in the dock were Thomas Pickles and Samuel Pickles (brothers) of Shafton, and Walker Pickles, of Ryhill, all three men being miners; and they had been in custody for several weeks, the cases having being adjourned from time to time. Articles alleged to have been stolen from the premises of the Midland Railway Company, included two lots of whisky (seventeen bottles and six bottles), three boxes of margarine, thirty-two packets of tea, six pairs of boots; from the Great Central Railway Company's premises, twelve bottles of wine, six stay bands, six bottles of Oxo; from Henry Lodge Ltd, a brass lubricator and from the New Monckton Colliery Company, a quantity of brass fittings, brass nails etc. Extensive evidence was provided before the justices retired, and on their return, the chairman, Dr Horne, said that the three men would have to go to prison for six months.

February 1918

By the beginning of the month a good deal of uneasiness was being expressed by local residents about the inclusion of horseflesh in the government schedule of rationed meat. Some newspapers gave publicity to a statement that horses were to be slaughtered for human food, giving rise to anxiety that horseflesh should be thrust upon the unwitting Barnsley public in place of beef. Inquiries made at the Ministry of Food by a press representative revealed the fact that it was not contemplated placing horseflesh on the market in large quantities at present. However, in order to reassure locals the *Barnsley Chronicle*, pointed out that there should be no alarm in confusing horseflesh for beef, as it is not only darker in colour and coarser in texture, but the fact that the horse has never been reared for public consumption in England, rendered supplies consequently scarce. Under the old law it was an offence to sell horseflesh for human consumption under the guise of beef, and strong measures would be taken against any tradesman who attempted to do so.

Official sources also revealed the reason why horseflesh is included in the schedule of rationed meats 'is to prevent the alien population from obtaining more than their fair share of flesh food. Few animals, except lame army horses are used for human food, and these are quickly consumed by the aliens and refugees, whose custom in their native lands is to eat horseflesh.'

On Wednesday, 13 February, a case of considerable interest to innkeepers and the beer drinking fraternity of Barnsley and district came before the Bench at Barnsley West Riding Police Court. Two licensees were heavily fined for breaches of the Beer (Prices and Descriptions) Order by selling 'fivepenny ale' at a price exceeding the legal charge. Evidence showed that both landlords, Henry Larkins, of the Sun Inn, South Hiendley and Joseph Greaves of the Pack Horse Inn, Royston on numerous occasions were seen to be charging 6d. a pint. Each were fined £5.

At the monthly meeting of the Barnsley Rural District Council on 13 February, the urgent need for houses at Carlton was emphasised, when a deputation of Carlton residents made a request to the Rural Council for the building of 200 houses as a matter of urgency. Mr F. Broadhurst, Carlton's representative on the rural council, said there were nearly 1,000 men working at Wharncliffe Woodmoor Colliery, 611 of whom lived outside the township, in Smithies, Monk Bretton, Mapplewell, Royston, Worsbrough and Cudworth; and 415 of the men came from the town of Barnsley itself. The time these men took walking to and from their work could be better utilised in such useful and productive activities as gardening.

In Carlton there was so great a shortage of houses that in many instances two families lived in one house. Mr Broadhurst said Carlton would continue to grow and no better building sites could be found anywhere than in the township. He desired to impress upon the council the desirability of preparing a scheme so that after the war they would be able to proceed with all possible speed. A letter from Wharncliffe Woodmoor Colliery Company was produced, stating that they would be pleased to do all in their power to assist the scheme for more adequate housing. Carlton had a population of 2,150 and there were 438 houses. After further discussion the council instructed the clerk to lay the requirements before the Local Government Board.

March 1918

At the beginning of the month it was widely reported that 'the Miners' Federation is giving earnest consideration to the government's call for 50,000 more men from the mines for army service'. The *Barnsley Chronicle* also reported:

'It transpires that the various mining areas have different opinions as to how the respective quota should be supplied. A proposal which may receive general assent is that the selection of the men should be by ballot... It will be interesting to see what is the men's [of Barnsley and District] decision as revealed by the ensuing ballot. No one who knows their superb record can question the true patriotism of our miners – patriotism strikingly demonstrated

not only by the number of men who have responded to the call of the colours and rendered heroic service at the front, but also by the splendid manner in which their comrades left in the pits have under conditions of special difficulty strenuously laboured to keep the nation's "home fires burning" and to maintain adequately the supplies of coal which are so vital for our munition works and other war purposes.'

On the evening of 12 March, the Mayor of Barnsley (Alderman H. Holden) presided over the monthly meeting of the Barnsley County Borough Council, when serious concerns were raised about the measles epidemic. The mayor said the outbreak had been severe, and the death-rate was almost appalling. Owing to the many rumours circulating that some households had lost four or five children, he would give the returns supplied by the medical officer. Up to Saturday, 9 March, 636 cases were notified or discovered and there had been 51 deaths, or about 8 per cent. They were doing all they could to check the outbreak. Three schools had been closed, and children under the age of 14 were being refused admission to houses of entertainment. There was no doubt that some parents were to blame for the lack of care shown by allowing their infected children to run about to other houses where there were no cases of measles, and also because of neglect in notifying the authorities of cases. Councillor Broley said he agreed with a great deal of what the mayor had said, but the relaxation of sanitary improvements in the town had a great deal to do with the epidemic and parents were not wholly to blame.

> **March 1918**
> **3rd**
> The Treaty of Brest-Litovsk was signed between Russia and Germany
>
> **23rd**
> Germany broke through on the Somme.

On another important matter, Alderman Raley, proposing the minutes of the Borough Development Committee, said Barnsley had done very well in the matter of allotments, but the national situation required that they should do even better. There were vacant allotments still available, owing to the increased land acquired by the council, and he hoped people would realise the necessity of providing as much as possible of their own food. During the last month they had let over 100 allotments, but they wanted to do even better this month.

Some stirring speeches were made at the Public Hall, Barnsley on the afternoon of Sunday, 24 March, to a meeting of the Licensed Retail Traders of Barnsley, in furtherance of the local War Bond Campaign for the supply of destroyers for the British navy. Councillor F. Goodyear presided, and the platform included the mayor, Lieutenant-Colonel

Hewitt and Captain Gill. The special aim of the gathering was to encourage local 'on and off' license holders to contribute investments to the value of £12,000, and at the end of the meeting it was announced that about £6,000 of this amount was already assured.

The mayor said Barnsley and District was asked to raise £150,000 for the purchase of a destroyer. So far they had raised £325,000 and he hoped they would make that into £450,000 for the purchase of three destroyers before the end of their campaign. It was not a case of giving, but was a good investment for the benefit of the investor and the country.

Easter was not a particularly pleasant one from a weather point of view, cold winds being accompanied by frequent showers of rain. In Barnsley and District the holiday passed quietly. Many of the collieries and workshops closed on Good Friday (29th), Easter Monday and Tuesday. Most people stayed at home. No special arrangements had been made for concessionary rail travel for the holiday and ordinary fares stood at 50-per-cent above pre-war prices. No temptation was offered for visits to the seaside or other pleasure resorts. At all the local churches on Easter Sunday there were large congregations, and on Monday the annual vestry meetings took place. Barnsley Market Place on Monday and Tuesday, was the rendezvous for the usual fair and feast attractions, where despite the inclement weather, large crowds flocked.

Barnsley Football Club's Easter holiday games were both played at Sheffield. On Saturday they visited Bramall Lane (Sheffield United), where the ground was soft and the going heavy, and notwithstanding that United put in a couple of goals in the first twenty minutes, the Oakwell lads came with a final rush and won the match 3-2. Monday's game took the lads to Hillsborough, where they found the Sheffield Wednesday team far too strong for them. A gate of 10,000 people saw the home team beat the visitors 6-2.

April 1918

On Friday, 5 April, the Mayor of Barnsley, Alderman H. Holden, at a wind-up meeting of the Barnsley and District War Bonds Campaign, was delighted to announce that the confidence he had expressed in the borough and district securing a trio of destroyers was never shaken. Supported by the Executive Committee, including Lieutenant-Colonel W.E. Raley, Aldermen Rose and Rideal, Councillors Plumpton and Goodyear, Messrs Frank Wood, H.J. Wells, A. Clegg, D. Paul (secretary) and other gentlemen, his Worship announced that the astonishing sum of £457,263 10s. 6d. had been realised. The mayor said he could not find adequate words to thank the executive committee for the invaluable help they had given him. Colonel Raley said the committee owed a debt of gratitude to the bank managers, and Councillor Goodyear observed that the press, too, were entitled to their thanks, and he moved a vote of thanks to them. Alderman Rose seconded, the resolution was agreed to and a motion that the committee continue was unanimously carried.

On 8 April: the residents of Barnsley and District began their first experience of compulsory rationing under the government scheme. Meat, butter and margarine could now only be bought in the prescribed quantities. The public were informed, when the housekeeper goes

"RATION"-AL FOOD FOR THOUGHT.

STOUT PARTY: These ration cards are a dashed nuisance.
THIN PARTY: Are they? We didn't have any where I've just come from.
STOUT PARTY: Please name that happy place, sir!
THIN PARTY: *Ruhleben*—a prison camp in Germany.

shopping she or he must take their own, and, or, their family's cards for all the rationed commodities. In the case of butter or margarine, the shopkeeper must cancel the square for the week. In the case of meat, the retailer has to tear off the necessary coupons. What was brought home to local people was that the meat rationing system was quite different for that of butter or margarine. They were told, beef, mutton or pork can only be bought at a butcher's where the purchaser must have registered. Any other meat a person can buy anywhere, but he must produce his cards, and the retailer must tear off coupons equivalent to the purchases. It is essential to remember that a person has only four coupons to use in a week. With three only of these, butcher's meat can be purchased. The fourth can be applied to the purchase of bacon, rabbit, poultry, corned meat or sausages. An important point to be noted is that every holder wishing to use it for buying bacon (including ham) must register it with the shopkeeper from whom he

**April 1918
9th**
Germany started and offensive in Flanders.

wishes to make his purchases. Further restrictions will apply from 5 May.

On Sunday, 14 April, the scheme for the rationing of meat supplies came into operation in the north of England. In the lead up to this active steps were taken by the Livestock committee and the Food Control Committees to ensure an equitable distribution of the supplies that are available, and butchers in Barnsley had a busy time preparing the rationing cards. All cattle markets throughout Yorkshire became regarded as either local or distributing centres. Yorkshire industrial areas were allotted markets from which they would draw their supplies, for instance, Leeds to Tadcaster and Wetherby, Sheffield to Driffield and York; and Barnsley to Malton and Goole.

In the Saturday, 20 April edition of the *Barnsley Chronicle* an article appeared under the banner:

THE MINING INDUSTRY AND THE NEW MILITARY SERVICE ACT:

'To the people of Barnsley and the West Riding it is of special interest that apart from the numbers expected to be yielded by the new Military Service Act, the Government is in addition to the recent demand for 50,000 recruits from the mines, now calling for yet another 50,000 men from this industry. Consequently the comb-out now in progress among our miners is for the considerable number of 100,000 men. No wonder the country is asked to economise in coal and the householders and other consumers of gas or electricity are being rationed in their use of these 'illuminants'. The position is undoubtedly serious. Mr Lloyd George in his recent statement in the House of Commons said having entered into the matter very carefully, he was satisfied that these men can be spared without endangering the output of coal essential for national industries. The Premier acknowledges that the miners are loyally meeting the present demand for more men, and he is confident that they will respond to the further call upon them in the same spirit, seeing how great is the national emergency...

Eligible men are also being winnowed out from munition works, and already about 100,000 have been obtained from that source. None too soon it has been decided to draw into the Army the young men still engaged in the civil service. There is to be a "clean cut" of these fit young men under 25 and a comb-out beyond

that age. Under the Military Service Act passed last January the
government are now cancelling all occupational exemption by age
blocks in certain specified industries. This is a practical and timely
application of the "clean cut."

...The government are undoubtedly obtaining from Parliament
extraordinary powers, for under the new measure, except in the case
of the conscientious objectors, the cabinet can by proclaiming that
a national emergency has arisen cancel at a stroke any and every
certificate of exemption and call to the colours every able-bodied
man up to the age of fifty-five, simply in virtue of a parliamentary
resolution. This augmented power to cancel exemptions Mr Lloyd
George has frankly told Parliament is yet another means of
effecting the "clean cut." It is a Draconian power, and what is
more if the military situation becomes more acute, there may be
no alternative than to courageously use it...'

May 1918

Sunday, 5 May, as from this day the holder of a ration card will, according
to official notification, be only able to buy bacon from the shopkeeper
with whom the card is registered, so the residents of Barnsley and
District were informed; and furthermore, only two coupons instead of
three may be used for butcher's meat, the third being available for bacon
and miscellaneous meats. Large supplies of bacon are expected to arrive
from America soon and will shortly be available for consumption. A
further reason for this change is to allow an opportunity for fattening
cattle on the coming season's grass. Yet another change – one designed
to secure a better diet for children – is the regulation allowing them on
reaching the age of 6 to have full rations, and boys over 13 are until they
reach the age of 18, permitted to receive a supplementary allowance
of bacon. The reason girls are not included in this scheme is that it is
considered that they do not as a rule eat as much as boys. Parents may
exchange a child's card for an ordinary card for full rations at the Local
Food Committee's offices.

On 11 May: the *Barnsley Chronicle* reported that Silkstone village
children have recently sent 218 fresh eggs to the national egg collection
for wounded soldiers and sailors.

Barnsley Borough was 'out of bounds' on account of the measles
epidemic, for the wounded 'Tommies' at Lundwood Hospital, we are
requested to say that should any party of local ladies and gentlemen
desire to entertain the deserving lads at the hospital they may make

application to the Matron, Miss Wombill. At present the wounded soldiers are debarred from attending any entertainments in Barnsley.

Tuesday, 14 May: at the monthly meeting of the council at Barnsley Town Hall, Alderman Rideal stated it was found necessary during the first few weeks of the working of the meat rationing scheme, in order to prevent the perishing of certain kinds of foodstuffs, to issue licences to local traders to sell without coupons at certain times in the week. Strong representations were made by the executive officer to the Ministry of Food with the request that these articles, such as tripe, brawn and edible offals, should be removed from the compass of the Meat Rationing Scheme. Alderman Rideal said that the Ministry of Food have now confirmed that this course will be followed and there will no longer be the fear that the wastage of foodstuffs will be caused by the operation of the scheme. Alderman Rideal added that supplies of meat under the Scheme in the last few weeks has been satisfactory and sufficient to meet the rationed demands of the Borough and the out-districts. The supply of butter has been more liberal than during the last few months and prospects for the future supply are very bright.

On 16 May: in a circular to the local education authorities, the Minister of National Service states that a further call must be made upon the public educational service, and all teachers and educational officials who were liable to military service under the Military Service (No 2) Act, 1918, and are in Grade 1, also those under the age of thirty-two on 1 January, 1918, who are Grade 2, will be called to the colours forthwith.

Magnificent weather favoured the Whitsuntide holidays in Barnsley and District, which have been spent by the majority of people at home, the facilities offered for travelling by rail or road being reduced to a minimum. On Whit Monday and Tuesday, thousands of people flocked into Barnsley, and on both these days there was a large influx of people to Stainborough and other local places of interest. At Shaw Lane on Monday the Barnsley cricket team just succeeded in defeating Grimethorpe.

June 1918
During the last few weeks by far the greater percentage of butcher's meat for sale throughout the country has been 'foreign'. This state of affairs has been brought about by government authorities requesting that English cattle should be given the chance to feed on the land during the summer months, a step which will ensure a supply of home-produced meat during the autumn and winter months.

On Friday, 7 June, Mr Arthur Bentley, president of the Barnsley and District Retail Butcher's Association, revealed that the position this coming week will be such that not an ounce of fresh-killed meat will be distributed in the Barnsley area, which includes the County Borough, Darfield, Ardsley Billingley, Wombwell, Hoyland, Birdwell, Worsbrough, Dodworth, Monk Bretton, Mapplewell, Royston and Cudworth.

Mr Bentley said, 'This week our association has been paid a visit by the Livestock Commissioner through whom the Barnsley and District supply is delivered, and he told us distinctly that for a few weeks hence at least the supply of foreign meat here will far exceed the quantity of English meat.'

Mr Bentley also said,

'From my own personal knowledge we have had our full quota of English meat in the past, and no district has been better catered for in that respect. Our Association is fully alive to the gravity of the situation and they have left no stone unturned in their efforts to move the powers that be to increase our supply. More than that we cannot do. The action of the government authorities in steadying the slaughter of English cattle is a well-meaning one as the people will find out when the cold weather comes along.'

The commissioner was loud in his praises of the Barnsley and District Association for the admirable way in which they had managed this difficult problem in the past, and he said he was confident of their loyalty in the future. Roughly 120,000lbs of foreign meat will be received in Barnsley this weekend and distributed throughout the town and district.

On Friday, 14 June, Mr Arthur Bentley, speaking on behalf of his Association, as president, informed the press that a scheme has been evolved whereby the public will have the privilege of purchasing English beef and mutton, periodically. Complaints – altogether ill-founded – have been made that the scheme which has been in operation for some months past, has

A CLEAN SWEEP!

JACK : " And the next job ? "

April was a busy month for the Royal Navy. A "sweep" of the Kattegat resulted in the destruction of 10 German mining craft. Later there were useful operations in the Bight of Heligoland. On St. George's Day the Dover Patrol made a glorious raid on the U-boat lairs at Ostend and Zeebrugge (*see page 1*). At the moment the Navy is waiting, with all the confidence and determination expressed by our artist in the cartoon, for its next job.

favoured the County Borough, and the Barnsley and District Retail Butcher's Association have determined that in the distribution to be made now the out-districts shall have first opportunity of getting supplies. Last on the list comes the County Borough of Barnsley. 'All that the Association is out for is to see to an equitable distribution of any meat received, and I can assure you that up to now that policy has been honestly carried out, despite the assertions which have been made in certain quarters,' said the president.

On the afternoon of Tuesday, 25 June, the Barnsley County Tribunal dealt with fifty-three appeal cases, the whole of the appellants being over 40 years of age and either in Grades 1 or 2. The sitting was held at the Town Hall, the Mayor (Alderman J. Holden), presided and was supported by Lieutenant-Colonel Raley, Aldermen Rose and Rideal and Councillor J. H. Cotterill.

When the court assembled Lieutenant-Colonel Hewitt (National Service Representative) said he would like to say a word with respect to men from 41 to 51 years of age. It was not the intention of the government to put any of these men into the fighting line, and men up to 45 would be used for garrison duty. Grade 1 did not necessarily mean that they were A1, or that they would be trained as A1 men, but consideration would be given to men of sedentary and other occupations and they would be trained according to their physical condition. There was considerable laughter when the mayor commented, 'I wish we could place confidence in the government Colonel Hewitt, but they change their mind so often.'

After these cases had been heard, one military appeal came up. Colonel Hewitt asked that William Guest, chimney sweep, 37, married, Grade 1, should be sent into the army. Guest said he had eight children, whereupon Colonel Raley said, 'Why his allowance will be that of a Field Marshal!', a comment which provoked much laughter. The military appeal was allowed and William Guest ordered to sign up.

'TO THE WOMEN OF ENGLAND. The fields are ripening for the sickle, the toil of the winter and the spring is earning its reward.

This is no ordinary harvest; in it is centred the hope and the faith of our soldiers that their own heroic struggle will not be in vain. In the days before the war the whole world was our granary. Now, not only are thousands of men fighting instead of tilling our own fields, but the German submarines are trying to starve us by sinking the ships which used to carry to our shores the abundant harvests of other lands.

> **June 1918**
> **25th**
> Mr Lloyd George issued the following appeal to women:

Women have already served the Allies by their splendid work upon the farms, but the Army in France has asked for still more men from the land to come and help their brothers in the desperate battle for freedom. These men must go; women will be first to say it. But the harvest is in danger for the want of the work these very men would have done.

Once again, therefore, as often before, I appeal to women to come forward and help. They have never failed their country. Yet they will not fail her at this grave hour.

There is not a moment to lose. Every woman who has the great gifts of youth and strength, if not already devoting these to essential work for her country, should resolve to do today. If she lives in a village let her go out and work in the fields from her home. If she can give her whole time, let her join the ranks of the Land Army. From the nearest Employment Exchange she can learn all about the conditions of service.

I have watched with deep interest and admiration the splendid work already done. Never have British women and girls shown more capacity or more pluck. And just as the soldiers have asked for thousands more men to come and help them to win the war, so do these brave women in the villages and in the Land Army call to other women to come and help them save the harvest.

I know this appeal will be heard. Ask the women who have already shown the way what they feel, they will declare that work in the fair fields of our great island is a privilege as well as a duty.'

July 1918

Major General Sir Frederick Maurice, KCB, referred to the importance of air power when writing in the *Daily Chronicle* on 1 July:

'If we have superiority in the air, which we certainly have, it is not yet as complete as we want it to be, and as it will be. I am very far from under-rating the importance of carrying the war into Germany by every possible means, and I fully appreciate the great moral effect

which the bombing of German towns will produce, when the people of Germany see that decisive military success is not within their power. But bombing raids, however numerous will not convert defeat on the battlefield into victory, and if we allow misplaced enthusiasm to divert aerial force from the battlefield in order to carry out distant enterprises into Germany we shall certainly suffer.

At present the prime duty of the Air Forces in France is to co-operate with their comrades on the ground in defeating the enemy. They have to act as the eyes of our generals and to blind the enemy; without them much of our long-range artillery would be useless, and while directing our own fire, they have to prevent the enemy from directing his; they have to harass and disturb, the enemy's concentrations behind his lines, and to interfere with his movements by damaging his communications.

Lastly, they have to co-operate directly in the destruction of the enemy's force in battle by flying low and shooting into the enemy's columns. Until we are absolute and unquestionably in all these various departments of aerial warfare we cannot afford to divert aerial strength from them in order to carry the war into Germany. This does not mean that we should neglect long-distance bombing, but that it should be given its place of our air plans as a whole.

We have now, and have for a long time past, a superiority in the air at the front, but we have always had to fight hard for it has never, since the battle of the Somme, been a great superiority. We bring down more of the enemy's aeroplanes than he brings down of ours, which means that he has greater difficulties than we have in finding out what is going on behind the front, and in directing the fire of the long-range guns. But the enemy does interfere with our reconnaissances, and he does bring off surprise blows.

It is as certain as anything can be in war that the Allied superiority in the air will develop steadily. Our own output of aircraft has not yet reached its maximum, and that of America has hardly begun to make itself felt. America has discovered that the standardisation and rapid production of aircraft, on a scale such as had been achieved in the case, say, of motor-cars, is not yet possible, and that early forecasts have not materialised, but she is putting the matter right with her accustomed energy, and we have had within the last few weeks the first American air communiqués and the first report of an American air raid into Germany.

Germany, even when she was free to bring all her air forces from the Russian front, could not obtain superiority against the incompletely developed air forces of the Entente, it is therefore certain that when the full output of the aircraft factories of the Allies begins to take shape we shall have everywhere on the Western Front, both in bombing and in every other branch of aerial activity, such a superiority as we had in the battle of the Somme, and this as far as can at present be foreseen will be one of the first steps towards final and complete victory.'

Send the Huns a Bomb from

WOMBWELL

ALL this week, men, women and children—your own friends and neighbours and fellow-citizens—have been hurrying to lend their money to their country, and thus help the men who are fighting for them. Join the throng of patriotic investors. Share in the success of Aeroplane Week.

By closing time to-night hundreds and thousands of pounds will have been lent towards the grand total which Wombwell means to invest this week in National War Bonds and War Savings Certificates.

Wombwell's Own AEROPLANE

That is to be the prize of success—the name of "Wombwell" on Our Aeroplane—the name that will remind our Yorkshire lads at the Front how Wombwell lent money to help them.

Draw your savings and invest to-day. The Huns will feel the power of *your* money when the Aeroplane "Wombwell" comes swooping down to spray their massed ranks with death from its machine-gun; or when the drone of its engines and the crash of its bombs resound through the cities beyond the Rhine.

Don't delay. The end of Aeroplane Week will soon be here. No sum can be too large. But do not think that your help is not required even if you can only lend a few pounds or shillings. Every sixpence counts.

Buy **National War Bonds** **to-day**

and **War Savings Certificates**

On 8 July: at the monthly meeting of Worsbrough Urban District Council, the Clerk, Mr J. Clegg, explained in detail the provisions of the Household Fuel and Lighting Order, under which the public are to be allowed a certain amount of coal, electricity or gas in accordance with the number of rooms occupied. The council were asked to appoint a Fuel Overseer and a Fuel and Lighting Committee to carry out the order in the township. In many districts, said the clerk, it would be a serious tax on someone's energies, but in the Worsbrough township there was so much home coal for colliery workers that there would not be a great amount of work, as there were practically no coal merchants. He pointed out that the Order did not interfere in any way with supplies of home coal. The salary of the Fuel Overseer was based on the number of houses in the township. Two-thirds would be paid by the Local Government Board and one third by the council. In the course of the discussion, Mr Littlewood said it would be a likely situation for a discharged soldier. It was decided to advertise the appointment at a salary of £120 per year.

On 9 July: the Allotments Committee of Dodworth Urban District Council, having viewed the allotments, formed the opinion that they were in as good a state of cultivation now as they had ever been. They made certain suggestions such as the raising of the fence wall a foot at Snow Hill and repairs to the plots at the top end of Jermyn Croft, and these were approved by the council. Mr Wills asked if anything had been done to obviate the damage done to allotments by trespassing. The chairman said the best way is to get hold of those responsible and summon them. Mr

**July 1918
15th**
The Second battle of the Marne began. The start of the collapse of the German army began.

Tarrent said that warning notices were being put up.

On Monday, 15 July, at the ordinary monthly meeting of the Education Committee, Lieutenant-Colonel W.E. Raley, the chairman, made reference of the calling up for military service of certain head teachers in Barnsley. Colonel Raley said he desired to refer to what was said the other day at the tribunal, and he desired to preface his remarks by saying that there was not a single head teacher in Barnsley who was serving with His Majesty's Forces. And then said:

> *'When we started some time ago the idea of the Teachers and Staffing Committee and ourselves too, was that, too, was this, that so far as we were concerned we would keep back no male teacher where there was another male teacher in a school. There is only one school in the town which has one male teacher only and that is St John's Boys School...We call upon other people with tremendous responsibilities to do it [join up] and we should be prepared to allow our teachers to go if we think fit or the Board calls upon us...'*

On 20 July: the advertisement which appeared in the *Barnsley Chronicle* a week ago signed by the Barnsley and District Milk Dealers' Association, caused a mild sensation throughout the district. The Association intimated to the general public that in consequence of the reduction of the controlled price of milk from 7d. to 6d. a quart, they would refuse to deliver milk in the town and certain out-districts after Monday last. As a result of this high-handed action many families in Barnsley and neighbourhood have this week been without milk, and the far reaching consequences of this particularly where families are composed of young children, have been seriously considered by the authorities. The powers vested in the authorities are drastic, and unless the dealers can make out a good case for the action they have taken it would not be surprising if the whole of the milk in the district was commandeered and distributed through a central agency. During the ensuing days a public enquiry took place at the Town Hall, before Mr J.A. Greene, Divisional Food Commissioner. After protracted discussions an arrangement was arrived at and in accordance with the commissioner's request, the farmers and milk dealers of the district promptly met together and decided to resume delivery of milk on Saturday morning.

On 22 July: the War Office announced that in view of the number of cases which have come to notice of men wearing chevrons and wound stripes to which they are not entitled, it is the intention of the authorities

Captured German soldiers march past a line of advancing Allied troops.

to take proceedings against all persons found to be offenders in these respects.

August 1918

On 1 August: there was much talk in Barnsley and District, when news got round about the President of the Board of Trade's (Sir Albert Stanley's) speech in the House of Commons the previous day. Sir Arthur stated that the shortage of coal for export and home use was due in part to the decrease in output of coal arising from the recruitment of miners and in part to increased demands by our Allies. The customary number of days worked per week at collieries in certain districts was less than six, but the number of districts to which this applied was less than it was before the war. At the present time a certain number of miners now in the Home Army, of low medical category, were being released to return to work, but the number available for release was limited. The executive of the British Miners' Federation had pledged themselves to the prime minister to use all their influence to get the miners to improve the output and to work regularly. He doubted if any substantial relief would be secured if the Miners' Eight Hour Act were suspended. It would be quite true to say that the decreased output in a measure is due to the decreased output per miner, but it should be borne in mind that the men left in the mines, taking them on the average, have not the degree of physical fitness that prevailed prior to the war.

On 4 August: magnificent weather favoured the garden party held in the grounds adjoining Dodworth Hall, and a large crowd patronised the event. Various kinds of sport was indulged in and a happy time was spent. The Dodworth Prize Band delighted the assembly with choice selections of music. The proceeds of the garden party will be devoted to the funds of the 1st Volunteers Battalion of the York and Lancaster Regiment (Barnsley).

On 17 August: this week the details of the annual report was released by Mr W. Walker, Acting Chief Inspector of Mines. A total of 1,021,340 persons were employed in and about the mines of Great Britain and Ireland under the Coal Mines Act during 1917. In the preceding year the number was 998,063. While the miners increased last year, the number of mines at work decreased from 2,847 to 2,814. In and about the mines under the Metalliferous Mines Act, 20,500 persons were employed. The number of mines decreased from 468 to 452. In and about the coal mines in 1917 there were 1,370 deaths due to accidents, and there were 25 deaths from accidents in the metalliferous mines.

On 24 August: at the monthly meeting of Wombwell Urban District Council earlier in the week, a problem that had been a bone of contention in recent months was discussed in the hope that a satisfactory resolution could be achieved. The matter of milk supply and its distribution was the 'burning issue'. Mr Mellor said that the council will recommend the Food Controller for permission to put the Milk Requisition Order 1917, into operation to enable the committee to buy milk from the producers who supply Wombwell, and also to retail it to the people with a view to bringing about an equitable distribution of milk in the district. Mr Mellor pointed out that a shortage of milk affected the public health vitally, and that was a matter which could not fail to be the concern of a public health authority. It was the duty of the council, therefore, to see that while there was a shortage of milk its effect on the public health should be mitigated as far as possible by equitable distribution.

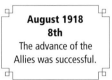

**August 1918
8th**
The advance of the
Allies was successful.

On 31 August: the *Barnsley Chronicle* reported that the second Barnsley Feast Charities' Carnival proved once again 'a glorious success', the proceeds of which amounting to £1,000 are to be equally divided between the Beckett Hospital, the Barnsley Patriotic Fund, the Mayor's Sailors' and Soldiers' Comforts Fund, and the Local Prisoners of War Fund. This decision to divide a portion of the receipts amongst our brave lads who are prisoners of war has 'given universal pleasure and satisfaction.'

Feast Week, by associating it with a carnival gave a new lustre to the festivities, which not only assured the people of Barnsley and the wide surrounding district a highly enjoyable holiday but also served as a truly patriotic purpose of providing the monetary means of providing comforts for prisoners of war belonging to Barnsley and the neighbourhood, replenishing the locally administered War Funds and materially supporting that deserving institution, the Beckett Hospital.

September 1918

On Monday, 2 September, an important meeting of employers, principally of the coal industry, was held at Barnsley and was addressed by Lieutenant-Colonel Joseph Hewitt, JP. The question of 'slacking' in the form of absenteeism at the pits was closely considered and suggestions for remedying the evil also formed a topic of debate. Many complaints were, it was said, to be heard from miners and others about the shortage of beer, but it was pointed out that the increasing need for saving all supplies of grain for food purposes was the primary cause of steadying the beer supply, and until the grain problem was mastered the workers must not expect any further concessions for the time being.

Colonel Hewitt referred to the fact that at the present time a supreme effort was being made by the Allies on the Western Front, and it was up to every man at home to put forth all the energy he could to assist in maintaining that effort until a decision was reached – first by providing all the munitions needed for warfare – and secondly maintaining the prime essentials for munitions, namely the output of coal. It should be borne in minds that for many months past we had been supplying the Allied forces with coal, and were it not for that fact the inevitable result that some of our Allies would have dropped out of the conflict.

No Britisher would desire that this should be; on the contrary, Colonel Hewitt said that he was sure their one sincere and fervent wish was that the 'Hun forces should be smashed as early as possible.'

Colonel Hewitt went on to say:

The question of absenteeism at the pits is not only deeply concerning employers, but the Government, and I deplore the fact that in the latest return I have received this morning absenteeism is shown as being over 20 per cent. It is incomprehensible to any loyal subject that such a state of things should exist in a country like our own and I am firmly convinced in my own mind that it is due to the unaccountable apathy which seems to pervade the minds of some men. Everything conclusively pointed to the fact that for household purposes there should be a shortage of coal during the ensuing winter, and this, added to the present decreased output and the demand for coal for war purposes, the Admiralty and the Allies, made the position look anything but pleasant. Careful sifting of the absentee question revealed evidence that the chief offenders were young and irresponsible miners, young fellows who appeared utterly callous and indifferent to the effect which their own self-indulgence caused to their brothers who were fighting at the front; and it would appear desirable to extend the principle which the Government had enunciated in the withdrawal of military exemption certificates of those who were 'slackers' and offer them the choice – work or fight.'

Averting to the important question of food, and the controversy which had been going on regarding beer supply, Colonel Hewitt mentioned that at an interview with the prime minister and Mr Bonar Law last week, he was personally assured by Mr Lloyd George that the principal points anxiously discussed by the Cabinet, and indeed all through the crisis, were supplies and tonnage. No question of temperance scruples or other extraneous matter had entered into their deliberations when discussing these all-important questions, and the prime minister laid stress on the fact that the Americans were actually depriving themselves of bread one day per week in order that the grain from their country may be sent over here; and they in this country could depend upon it, that the Americans would not make such a sacrifice as this if they knew that the grain was being shipped to England for the purpose of making beer.

This, concluded Colonel Hewitt, was a matter which the entire public should take seriously to heart and should have due effect upon those who were disposed to call out for more beer. What the Cabinet were out for was to win the war, and it was only by such sacrifices as these that the ultimate goal of victory could be secured. Colonel Hewitt added that he had the utmost faith in the Yorkshire miners setting the example to their fellow workers during the next few months of anxiety, by keeping hard at their work and showing the government and the lads at the front that they were doing their level best to hasten the end of this terrible war.

On 14 September: one week after reports of the meeting with employers concerning absenteeism, concerns were still being raised prompting the *Barnsley Chronicle* to include the following article in its next edition:

USING THEM UP.

THE KAISER:—"Hindenburg, it's going out, bring some more coal."
HINDENBURG:—"All Highest, you must be careful, this is all we have"

'Distinctly timely is the appeal to our miners for specially strenuous efforts to maintain the country's coal supplies, for coal is essential to success alike on the Western Front and on what may be called the Home Front. It is expressing only a truism to point out that we cannot possibly win the war without coal. That is why any miner who is a deliberate shirker is as much the enemy of his country as is the open traitor. The coal situation is more serious than some people realise. Things much indeed have come to an anxious pass when the position with regards to coal is officially described as "the worst crisis at home that we have had to face during this war" ... It is because our Yorkshire miners as a class are intensely patriotic that we believe Colonel Hewitt's stirring exhortation will have the desired effect now that the bedrock truth has been brought home to the men that by more regular attendance the deficient output of coal can to a great extent be made good... The Coal Controller's latest figures showing that in August the coal *output was 1,714,800 tons below that of the corresponding four weeks of last year, while the output of the first thirty-two weeks of this year reveals a deficiency of nearly 13,500,000 tons. What is particularly disquieting in the situation is that this serious shortage, as the Coal Controller observes, comes at a time when extra demands for many million tons of coal are being made upon him for the American Expeditionary Force, for the urgent military requirements of France and Italy, for the British Navy, and for the manufacture of munitions. It is not surprising that the Coal Controller's serious disclosures have led to an appeal to the War Cabinet to take urgent steps for dealing with the present very anxious coal situation. Meanwhile, if the chronic slackers among the miners will not work, their exemption certificates should be promptly withdrawn, and they should be sent into the fighting line, for obviously as fit young men of military age they have no right to be out of the Army except on the express condition that they loyally and strenuously do their bit in so essentially a key industry as coal mining.'*

On 21 September: regarding Barnsley's allotments and the secret of their success a journalist sought an answer from Councillor Plumpton:

'An old pressman alike as a food consumer and as an amateur gardener, it occurred to me a few days ago to make a friendly call on Councillor Plumpton, the chairman of the Old Town Food Production Show, and glean from him some of the secrets of its remarkable success, as publicly and strikingly evidenced at its recent exhibition of vegetables and other produce. I found the editor of the Barnsley Chronicle *pleasantly and helpfully communicative concerning the best methods of raising allotment produce of all kinds – an art in which Mr Plumpton has specialised, and respecting which he may therefore be regarded as an authority. We chatted for a time on the gratifying popularity of the allotment movement in Barnsley and the whole-hearted zeal in which every holder of a plot has done his bit at food production. The fact that still more allotments are available did not escape comment.*

"Please tell me," I said, "the kind of vegetables you would advise any new applicants to grow on local plots."

"Well," replied Mr Plumpton, "our experience shows that the vegetable of greatest dietetic value and those, moreover, especially suited to local soil are potatoes, onions, peas, runner beans and carrots. It is found that these vegetables are with reasonable care

and attention particularly productive. A Barnsley man with a plot of moderate area might very well select these vegetables for his principal crops, with the addition of a few rows of broad beans and some lettuces and radishes, and even leeks, if his taste runs that way. Cultivated on these lines, he would probably find his plot almost self-supporting nearly all the year round provided he also put in some winter greens, brussels sprouts and broccoli."

> **September 1918**
> **8th**
> The advance of the Allies was successful.
>
> **19th**
> Turkish forces collapsed at Megido.

"What about fertilisers?" I injected. "For my experience is that the average amateur trips up badly over soil conditions and fertilisers?"

"Yes, so I understand," remarked Mr Plumpton. "It is sometimes objected that artificial manures exhaust the soil by stimulating it to produce beyond its natural rate. This objection is, however, only a line of truth. The fact is the continued use of special manures such as sodium nitrate or lime do undoubtedly tend to exhaust soil because they do supply only one ingredient. The main fertilisers are phosphatic, potassic, calcareous and nitrogenous."

"I suppose that Barnsley allotment holders like those elsewhere, are thinking mostly in terms of potatoes."

"Yes, potatoes are our principal product, and for potatoes we can testify there is nothing like farmyard manure ploughed or dug in as deeply as possible, leaving the surface rough. Soot is time and part at the second hoeing; and a mixture of three parts of superphosphate of lime, one of nitrate of soda also applied at the second hoeing."

"It would be interesting I am sure, to have your opinion of the food value of the potatoes."

"On that important point I can speak most emphatically," remarked Mr Plumpton. "There is no doubt whatever that area for area the potato produces more immediate available food than can be obtained by any other means. For instance, it has been demonstrated that an acre of potatoes will feed twice the number of persons that an acre of cereal corn will feed. Unquestionably in this great food emergency every county should be self-supporting in its potato supply, and any district that is not growing its full quota will find it difficult hereafter to justify its neglect of what is obviously a high national duty..."

The interviewer said: "I certainly think that Barnsley has every reason to be proud of what has been so magnificently achieved by

Councillor Charles Plumpton, wearing his uniform after appointed Second Lieutenant for the First Barnsley Battalion. He was editor of the *Barnsley Chronicle* from 1909-1923.

its allotment holders, and especially of the timely and well directed stimulus given by the Committee of the Old Town Food Production Show. Anyone who walks through the food plots cannot fail to be amazed at the vast quantities of vegetables grown. The circumstances that the cultivators are now eating their own produce must make it easier to reduce the consumption of bread in their homes."

"Good luck then to the Barnsley allotments and to the Old Town Food Production Show," exclaimed the pressman.

...As a concluding word Mr Plumpton, with all the keenness of an enthusiast again emphasised the salient fact that food situation can only be saved by a great extension of the number of allotments. It is a remarkable fact, he said, that whereas a comparatively short time ago this country only produced one fifth of its food needs, it now produces four fifths, thus leaving only one fifth to be brought overseas. This great and gratifying achievement is largely owing to the increased number of allotments. If now in Barnsley and elsewhere a further spurt be made, the additional allotments combined with the special efforts of the farmers may make this country for the first time in its modern history, absolutely independent of outside food supplies. Locally, as Mr. Plumpton aptly pointed out, the outstanding fact that now is pre-eminently the time when applications should pour in for allotments so that there may be adequate opportunity for the preparation of the land for record crops next year.'

On 24 September: at a meeting of the Yorkshire Miners' Association at Barnsley, Mr Herbert Smith, JP, president, said the council had instructed the officials to open negotiations with the South and West Yorkshire coalowners for the discussion of rules for appointing committees to increase output. The miners were anxious to do all they possibly could, and were pleased to see that Lord Aberconway agreed that the miners as a body were doing all that they possibly could to increase the output, and also that the shortage was caused by the National Service taking away 75,000 'Grade 1' men from the pits in face of advice to the contrary. It was impossible,

Mr Smith added, that men aged 40 and 50 could attempt to tram corves [wagons] and deal with transport generally in the pits as efficiently as the younger men. These were the class of men drawn away from the pits, hence the reduction of the output, but, as Lord Aberconway stated, the output per man was larger now than was the case prior to the war.

October 1918

On Wednesday, 9 October, at the Barnsley West Riding Police Court, Herbert Lindley, bookmaker, from Hoyland, was summonsed for keeping a gaming house; and Ethelda Lindley (his wife), Harold Vickers, miner, James Sherrington, chemical worker, and John Jackson, miner, all of Hoyland, were also charged with 'aiding and abetting'.

Sergeant Greenwood said that on Tuesday, 10 September, he and PC King were concealed near Belmont House (the residence of the Lindleys) and they had a good view of the back door and the greenhouse. At 9.30 am he saw a man hand a slip of paper to Mrs Lindley, and this was repeated by two other men. At 11am Mrs Lindley went into the greenhouse and between that time and 3.30 pm they saw thirty-five men, two women, a boy and a girl go to the greenhouse. Herbert Lindley joined his wife in the greenhouse and remained there some time, during which time several men went there.

The next day the witnesses saw several men go to the back door of Belmont House and Herbert Lindley handed something to each man, which appeared to be money, which the men counted and put in their pockets. Mrs Lindley was also seen handing two men money. Later that afternoon the Lindleys were in the greenhouse where thirty-five men and two women went there and handed them betting slips. The same thing took place the following day.

Inspector Brimms spoke as to having raided Belmont House where a mass of betting material was recovered and all the people in the dock were present at the time. One sheet of paper showed 250 bets amounting to £44 15s. 6d. Slips and telegrams bore names of horses running that week at Newmarket.

Having listened to a considerable amount of evidence the magistrates retired and upon returning to court the chairman said they considered the whole of the cases proved, except in the case against Vickers, who would be discharged. Herbert Lindley was fined £100 (the maximum fine) or six months imprisonment; his wife was fined £10 and the other defendants £3 each. 'We feel it our duty to inflict severe penalties in these cases, considering the present state of the country and the fact, too, that practically young children have been encouraged to gamble,' concluded the chairman.

On Saturday, 12 October, Barnsley Football Club travelled to Bradford with a weak side – Donkin being one of the absentees. They were trounced by City to the tune of 8 goals to 1. A crowd of over 3,000 watched the match. At the outset Barnsley forced the pace. And Newton twice was very near scoring. In the first place Wilkinson saved brilliantly, and a moment later was fortunate to stop a low shot with his foot. These attacks were not long sustained, and the game subsequently ran in favour of Bradford City.

At a meeting at the Pitt Street Wesley Guild, on Tuesday, 22 October, Mr W.S. Purchon, MA, of Sheffield University gave an interesting address to a representative audience on the 'Housing Problem.' The chair was taken by Councillor H.M. Walker, who in the course of his remarks said the housing problem was one which concerned the physical and moral well being of the inhabitants of this country. They were told that a quarter of a million dwellings were needed and that provision must be made at once for the erection of these houses.

Mr Purchon said that he treated the problem from the point of view of the architect rather than as a politician or an economist. It did not matter to him so much who built the houses as they were so badly needed as that they should be suitably designed and well built. He hinted that higher rents would be called for from the artisan classes, but he thought they would be quite willing to pay such for suitable dwellings. There were no better designers of either large or small houses than are to be found amongst our own British architects, and as proof of this it was stated that very large numbers of houses had been built to the design of some of these gentlemen in America, France, Belgium and in Germany too. Much human life was sacrificed through the want of proper housing provision, especially infant life, and the health of many people who do not succumb to the effects of their unhealthy dwellings is impoverished. After pointing out the defects of back-to-back houses and dwellings with badly designed staircases, draughty rooms and lack of proper sanitary conveniences, the lecturer indicated some of his views as to the type of house that should be built. In conclusion, Mr Purchon advocated proper schemes for town planning that would be likely to last twenty years or more ahead.

At the end of the month many important points were put forward in the annual report on the health of the borough by Dr F.A. Sharpe, Medical Officer of Health. The report draws particular attention to the dearth of dwelling houses consequent upon the war. In a striking reference to the food question Dr Sharpe advised that the distribution of milk should be controlled by the local authorities.

The outstanding features during the past twelve months have been the absence of the usual infectious diseases, resulting in the lowest zymotic death rate for the past twenty-five years and a remarkable drop in the birth-rate. The total cessation of house building and the immigration of people into the borough has led to an amount of overcrowding, which is causing much anxiety.

October 1918
19th
Germany asked the Allies for an armistice.

29th
Germany's navy mutinied.

30th
Turkey made peace.

November 1918

On 2 November, the new coal rationing scheme began and at the end of the week a number of important provisions will take effect in the divisional area, which includes the whole of the West Riding. From the second of the month no delivery of coal, coke, or other fuel will be permitted unless the trader holds the certificate of the local Fuel Overseer in respect of the premises for which such delivery is intended.

On Wednesday, 6 November, at the Barnsley West Riding Police Court, the Wharncliffe Silkstone Colliery Company sought to recover £10 from John Levitt, a young miner, of Birdwell, for breach of contract. Mr W.M. Gichard, solicitor acting on behalf of the colliery, said the proceedings were taken with a view to impressing upon young men such as the defendant the importance of following their occupation regularly in these strenuous days. The defendant had been constantly absent from work and when spoken to by the management he replied, 'I may as well be frank – it is through idleness!' The Bench made an order for payment of the amount claimed.

On Saturday, 9 November, at noon the members of the Barnsley County Borough Council unanimously elected Alderman Lieutenant-Colonel W.E. Raley, JP, as mayor for the ensuing year. The *Barnsley Chronicle* reported the following:

'On Monday, 11 November, the news of the signing of the armistice was received with great rejoicings throughout the country, the pent up feelings of the nation finding expression in a unanimous and earnest outburst of enthusiasm. And on Monday morning, as the fateful hour fixed by Marshall Foch approached, the suspense was intense. In Barnsley, as in other towns, the news was awaited anxiously. From early morning the people about the streets

discussed the situation eagerly, and shortly after eleven o'clock when the joyous tidings came through that Germany had signed the Armistice, these same people gave vent to their pent up feelings in no uncertain way. Market Hill and Peel Square soon became heaving with crowds of people; and when the official declaration was made by printed poster on the windows of the Barnsley Chronicle *building in Peel Square, all doubts, if any existed, were set at rest.'*

And continued:

'It was amazing how quickly the news spread and astonishing to learn that virtually the whole of the mills and workshops closed to enable their workforces to join in the celebrations on this momentous day. In any event, the workers were too excited to continue their tasks, they swarmed into the streets and vigorously shook the hands of their friends. Flags, banners, bannerettes, bunting and all manner of patriotic items were hoisted where a building stood to hoist them; and the children dashed from schools singing their hearts out with unstifled joy. The bells of the parish church rang a merry peal and the entire town was given up to holiday. As evening approached, and the electric lamps in the streets were able, once again, to give of their best – the shades having been promptly removed by the Corporation staff, the thoroughfares became busier still, and right until the midnight hour people walked about the streets in cheerful mood.'

On 12 November: Tuesday evening, in the House of Commons, Barnsley's MP, Sir Joseph Walton, turned to another issue of greater concern to his constituents:

'We are told by the Minister of Reconstruction that it will take three, six, nine, or twelve months to change over many of the works of the country from war work to peace work. But I tell my Right Hon. friend the Financial Secretary to the Treasury of one business of vital importance to this country where there is no necessity for a day to be lost with regard to the change over, and that is a trade he knows a great deal about – the coal trade. Four hundred thousand coal

Alderman Lieutenant-Colonel W. E. Raley, JP.

miners volunteered to fight for their country. I ask the Government to release and bring back to this country immediately 100,000 coal miners from our fighting forces. By doing that they will secure that the people of the country shall live during the winter, which is near upon us, in well-warmed houses and in greater happiness and contentment. In doing that they will provide sufficient call for the works and manufactories and it will make all the possible difference in the matter of our financial and economic recovery. Not only ought they to bring back at once 100,000 coal miners, but they ought to follow that with no long delay by at least another 100,000... We should bring back skilled artisans, the managers of one-man businesses and indespensible men in various business undertakings who have been taken away and whose return would do an enormous amount to assist in the rapid getting back to peace work of the works they were connected with...'

> **November 1918**
> **3rd**
> Austria made peace.
>
> **9th**
> Kaiser Wilhemn II abdicates.
>
> **11th**
> Germany signed an armistice with the Allies – the official date of the end of the First World War.

The parents of an esteemed Barnsley military officer, who has spent a considerable time at the front, handed in a letter to the *Barnsley Chronicle*, for publication, which vividly described the state of things which exist in the battle zone of France, some extracts from which are included here:

'Monday and again yesterday I suspended all duties; to be candid, I both literally and actually, took French leave and visited the towns which have only recently been recaptured by very heavy fighting in the past few days. I have read with keen interest and deep emotion the descriptions in the newspapers of the spontaneous rejoicings at home and abroad. Making all allowances for the inadequacy of the written words and giving my imagination full play whilst so reading, I feel, beyond the telling, that it almost pales into insignificance with the inspired experiences I have had during the two days' tour. The country which I passed through is scarred heavily with the havoc of battle, so much so, that it actually caused a physical ache, and I found it very necessary to crush my imagination on the subject of the awful inferno that the inhabitants of the recent battle zone have been through. After four years of drastic treatment under captivity, for this last "hell phase" to visit them, is just as impossible for me to comprehend as to grasp the meaning of "The Universe." They were driven towards enemy

country by the terrifying intensity of our attacks enhanced by the bombardments of the enemy in his attempts to stop our advance. Nowadays, nothing lives while the tide of battle rolls over an area, not even insects or rats.

But yesterday, the picture I saw in every road, lane or track, of joy incarnate, was too overwhelming for collected thought or perfect observation. I cannot describe it, but I now have a faint idea of the meaning underlying the saying of "all men are alike when the depths in each of us is reached." The whole of the forward army transport was engaged in the work of "taking people home" from the enemy's lines. Though most of the homes are damaged, a big percentage wantonly, it did not detract me from the delirious yet supressed joy of everyone. Every class of vehicle was used in this very human work. I saw the Generals and other Staff Officers with their cars joyously overloaded with men, women and children, all accompanied by their precious bundles of intimate personal belongings. I saw our general with two dirty-nosed infants, wrapped in his greatcoat asleep, one in each arm, with the mother sitting between him and his Aide-de-Camp. The Aide had a small boy of about eight on his knee carrying a tri-colour. Grandfather sat next to the driver with a little girl standing between his knees with her face pressed against the wind-screen. Car after car, motor-lorry after motor-lorry, general service wagons, limber wagons, and even field guns, were transporting the recently unhoused people back to their desolate homes. This picture was

so overpowering that I frequently had to stop the car which I was driving through being temporarily blinded by irrepressible tears of joy. You may have seen many old masterpieces, in which the artist has painted what is described as a godlike, saintly or angelic expression, but which I prefer to classify as the 'intense human expression.' Well it is indelibly fixed in my mind for all time. It was on every face, so that every face became alike and everybody acted alike. Despite the bustle and joyous attempt to do a week's work in a day, it was all as gently and tenderly done, that looking back to it now, through the intervening few hours, it appears to one to be the commencement of 'the millennium.' Even the horses seemed to be infected and pulled their immense loads with a will through the heavy roads and I did not see one either whipped or spurred. Motor-lorry drivers even changed gear without the usual clash and clang. I saw one motor-lorry driver with about four tons of bread, on a three-ton lorry, for the civilians, entering a town with a look on his face which literally smiled at you – "I am God." Meeting this man was one of the occasions when I had to pull up through temporary blindness.

Last night I tried very inadequately to describe as I feel that I have failed in conveying to you, the joyous experiences I have had to the other officers of my Company, with the result that they have all gone forward from fifty to seventy miles to see and share in all this. I have been brought nigh to the belief of God in man and feel that whatever the future may hold I and my fellow-men have not lived in vain.'

December 1918

Prime Minister David Lloyd George had promised servicemen that they would return to a land 'fit for heroes to live in'. The harsh reality was, nothing could have been further from the truth. Civilians had also been through a gruelling time at home, while war was raging abroad, and they like the brave warriors returning home, were also struggling to come to terms with what had happened and the implications for the future were. Life in Great Britain would never be the same as it had been before the war.

The great homecoming brought with it a unimaginable horror, in the form of a devastating influenza epidemic during the winter of 1918-19. Known as Spanish flu, this lethal airborne virus, which affected every continent, became a global pandemic killing millions worldwide (far more than had been killed during the hostilities of the First World War, the exact number is not known but the deaths resulting directly from the virus have been cited as being as great as 50 million). The virus had found an ideal breeding ground in the fetid trenches and was spread by returning soldiers. The death toll was 228,000 in Great Britain alone. By the end of the pandemic, only one region in the entire world, an isolated island called Marajo, located in Brazil's Amazon River Delta, had not reported an outbreak of this deadly virus.

On the afternoon of Wednesday, 11 December, a conference of the Barnsley Rural Food Control Committee was held, presided over by Mr W. Kilby JP, during which the proceedings became somewhat lively after the subject of unfair practices regarding the fair supply and distribution of rationed meat. A letter had been received from Mr E. Grayson, a butcher from Carlton, complaining of the treatment he and other country butchers were receiving at the hands of the committee which managed the co-operative slaughter-house at Barnsley, where all cattle and sheep for the district were slaughtered and distributed. 'The Barnsley committee is ruining the country trade, and we cannot do justice to the people,' the letter stated, and the allegation was made that the borough meat could actually be obtained without coupons. The letter had been sent to Major Daltry, who replied that investigation should be made into the allegation.

Mr A. Hague, of Billingley, said that as a result of the complaint he had made at the last committee meeting, the butchers had now been summoned to the meeting, and as Mr Bentley, president of the Barnsley and District Retail Butchers' Association, was also present, it would be as well for the butchers present to speak their minds. Mr Grayson said it was impossible for the country dealers to pay their way owing to the treatment meted out to them. Only recently his own supply was made up with 5 stones of fry, and when he complained he was told to go. Mr Kilby asked, 'Do you mean to tell me that the Barnsley borough butchers are treated like that – Mr Bentley himself, or any one of them?' Mr Grayson was quick to reply with an emphatic 'No!' then added, 'The Barnsley butchers got a plentiful supply of the best meat and their customers 'swanked' about it.' He said he knew of individuals who came to the town and got meat without coupons. Mr Hague asked Mr Grayson, 'When you have got your meat home have you found that you were charged for more weight than you received?' Mr Grayson replied, 'Yes, it has occurred regularly. Only last week my mutton was 2lbs short. Mr Horbury, another Carlton butcher, complained that he had been generally charged 'first grade,' but during the last week or two he had done better. Mr Hague asked, 'Since the letter appeared in the paper?' to which Mr Horbury retorted, 'Yes. There is too much of the "private cupboard" to my liking.'

Another butcher described the dealings as being 'Secret chamber business.' Mr Horbury went on to say that he had got thoroughly sick of the treatment he had received, and unless there was a decided alteration he should give up butchering unless he did it for himself. Favouritism was shown week after week, and whether it was 'back-handism' he could not tell. He had paid as much as 1s. 7d. per lb for mutton, and it was time there was an alteration. The country butchers were nothing but scavengers! It was scandalous, for they were working for nothing. Some of the ewes they could read a newspaper through!

Mr Kilby asked Mr Horbury, 'Do you mean you mean to say you pay top grade price every time?' The reply quickly came back, 'Yes, and I have meat lately in my shop that before this "pool" business I would not have near, I have had nothing but "slippy old ewes" and some beef I would not have cut up before this.' Mr Helliwell, another village butcher, also complained of the quality of the mutton, and said he had never been supplied with a 'Welsh' sheep by the 'pool'. Many times his meat had not weighed out. When asked if he thought he was getting his fair share of first-grade mutton, Mr Helliwell replied that he had not had any first-grade mutton at all, only poor quality meat at first-grade prices.

There were many more complaints during the lengthy meeting along similar lines, following which Mr Hague then quoted a mass of figures, and went on to say that from the 'pool' unfit meat was sent to the country and the public were crying shame upon it. It was time there was a change and if it was possible he would move that they withdraw from the 'pool' and let the butchers distribute their own meat. At Carlton there were two excellent slaughter-houses, and also one at Billingley. Why should these tradesmen be compelled to put their money in the 'pool' and be treated in this fashion? Mr Horbury said, 'I have stood it while I am sick,' to which Mr Bentley entered into a long explanation, quoting official figures to combat those produced by Mr Hague, at the conclusion of which Mr Horbury was prompted to ask, 'Is this government

THE GREAT
PEACE BAZAAR
NOW ON IN THE
DRAPERY STORES
OF THE
Barnsley British Co-operative Society,
When the first Grand Display of Christmas Dolls, Toys, Books and Presents, will be made at
NEW STREET ISLAND CORNER,
BARNSLEY.

NOTE: For obvious reasons there will be a great demand for Christmas Goods of all kinds for this, the first "Peace Christmas" since 1913, and as supplies are limited, and repeats in most cases impossible, you should certainly BUY EARLY.

arrangement a secret business?' to which came back the reply from Mr Bentley, 'There is no secret whatever about it, and what the "pool" does is simply to carry out the instructions of the government.'

After further argument, Mr Bentley explained that the turnover at the 'pool' was £6,000 per week. The committee had every desire to deal equitably and fairly with all tradesmen, and if any complaints were made in writing these would be properly dealt with. Mr Hague at the conclusion of the conference moved a vote of thanks to Mr Bentley for his kindness in coming to offer an explanation, and expressed the hope that there would be no need for complaints in the future.

Christmas is traditionally a time for many happy reunions; such indeed, have taken place, but the dreadful toll of the war has told its inevitable tale and in not a few homes in Barnsley and District, Yuletide has recalled sad memories. Happily, however, the belligerent countries have ceased their battles, and the minds of the populace must now be centred upon the building up of a more happy and contented nation, In Barnsley, despite the fact that it was the first 'peace' Christmas, the festivity passed off very quietly. Preparatory to the 25th the shopkeepers appeared to do a roaring trade. Money was plentiful, as also was food, and the streets on Christmas Eve bore a bright and animated appearance. At several of the churches the customary midnight services were held, and with the weather being so favourable there were large congregations. At the several hospitals the inmates were given their usual Christmas 'Cheer' and naturally special efforts were made to make our wounded soldiers happy. In the past the sport-loving section of the community have usually had a feast of football; this year on account of the war the leagues have not been taken seriously and the interest locally of the doings of the 'Oakwellites' has waned. Still a fair number of supporters visited Rotherham on Christmas Day, and on Boxing Day the crowd at Oakwell was reminiscent of pre-war days.

Chapter Seven

1919: The Aftermath

New Year celebrations in Barnsley and district although somewhat muted compared to the celebrations in pre-war years, were conducted in the spirit of optimism and the fervent hope that what lay ahead in the future would be worth the sacrifices of so many.

January 1919
4th
Peace conference met at Paris.

21st
The surrendered German naval fleet at Scapa Flow was scuttled.

Thoughts soon turned to the improvements in various quarters that had been tentatively approached during the war years and the engines of local power were quick to turn to bring these changes to enhance the lives and living standards of the local population to a speedy reality. On 4 January, the monthly meeting of Barnsley Borough Council took place and was presided over by the Mayor, Colonel W.E. Raley. After other business had been discussed the clerk drew the members attention to a meeting that had taken place the previous day at which the Local Government Board's suggestion in respect of housing and planning schemes had been discussed, and recommended that the Town Clerk be authorised to communicate with the Urban District councils of Ardsley, Darton and Monk Bretton, suggesting the preparation of a joint housing scheme for the whole of the districts concerned.

The mayor moved the adoption of the minutes and intimated that he only wished to say a few words about this great question of housing. They all knew that as far as Barnsley was concerned the area of the county borough was very small indeed, in fact it had one of the smallest county borough areas within the United Kingdom. There were very few vacant places on which to build houses in suitable localities, and therefore, as they were bound to provide for the population of the borough something like 1,560 houses, it would be necessary for some of these houses to be built outside the borough boundaries... Alderman Rideal seconded, and the minutes were approved. And so the seeds were sown that sparked a programme of building that would be replicated throughout the whole of Barnsley and District; some local councils already having sown their own seeds to provide better housing on a scale never previously dreamed of or contemplated.

SPECIAL GRATIS SUPPLEMENT TO

The Barnsley Chronicle

AND PENISTONE, MEXBRO', WATH, AND HOYLAND JOURNAL.

VOL. LXI. NO. 3161. TUESDAY, MAY 27, 1919. GRAT

RETURN OF THE BARNSLEY BATTALIONS.

CADRE TO ARRIVE ON WEDNESDAY.

CIVIC WELCOME TO TAKE PLACE ON MARKET HILL.

COLOURS TO BE DEPOSITED IN ST. MARY'S CHURCH.

THURSDAY'S GREAT PROGRAMME.

Barnsley has had many memorable military gatherings and processions since the outbreak of hostilities, but they have all been to say good-bye and God-speed to our departing troops.

On Thursday next there will be another, a greater, and a happier procession and gathering on Market Hill.

It will be the day of days for Barnsley, for the inhabitants will at last be able to turn out to welcome back the Cadre and Colours of the 13th Battlion of the York and Lancaster Regiment.

The Battalion was quickly raised in September, 1914, in response to a call for volunteers to uphold their country's honour, and the town's farewell to this and its sister Battalion, the 14th, was made on Thursday, May 13th, 1915, when the "Pals" left Silkstone Camp for Cannock Chase.

None then knew when the local Battalions would return to the town which gave them birth, but few, we venture to think, when they saw their citizen-soldiers on that memorable march to Court House Station, thought that it would be four years to the very month before the members of the 13th Battalion would return victorious, and with colours flying.

The great day, long looked forward to, is at last in sight, and all Barnsley, we hope, will turn out to cheer the representatives of the Battalion, and the discharged and demobilised men who carried the Battalion with honour and glory through many weary months of war and hardship to the wonderful day of Victory.

The cadre of the 13th York and Lancaster Regt. (the original First Barnsley Battalion) arrived at Southampton on Thursday, and at present are at Catterick Bridge.

A telegram was received by the Town Clerk (Mr. W. P. Donald) on Friday, informing the Corporation that the cadre were prepared to come to Barnsley this week, and arrangements were at once made for their reception.

It has been arranged that the full cadre shall arrive in the town to-morrow (Wednesday) noon, and they will be accommodated at the Drill Hall, Eastgate. They will bring with them the King's Colours of the Battalion, presented to them when they went to form part of the Army of Occupation in Germany, and these have to be deposited for safe custody in the Barnsley Parish Church.

The ceremony in connection with the depositing of the Colours will take place on Thursday at 12 noon.

The proceedings will begin at 10.30 a.m., when the discharged and demobilised men of the 13th and 14th Battalions will assemble in the Queen's Grounds. Each Battalion will be inspected by its former Commanding Officers. The inspection, it is hoped, will be carried out by Major-General Hulk (formerly commanding the 14th Battalion), Col. Sir Joseph Hewitt, J.P. (formerly commanding the 13th Batt.), and Col. W. E. Raley, J.P. (formerly commanding the 14th Batt.)

Shortly before 11 a.m., the cadre will march off from the Drill Hall to the Queen's Grounds, and from there they will head the procession of the two Battalions to Market Hill.

Here the cadre and the Battalions will be received by the Mayor (Col. W. E. Raley, J.P.), and members of the Town Council, and His Worship will formally welcome back the men to the town.

The Battalions will move off from Market Hill to St. Mary's Church, and will then form a guard of honour through which the Council and the cadre will proceed to church.

At the Church door they will be met by the Rector (Rev. Canon Hervey, M.A.), and a short service will be held, during which the Colours will be formally handed over to the Rector by Major Goodburn, the officer at present commanding the 13th Battalion.

After the ceremony, the two Battalions will march to the Queen's Grounds, where refreshments will be served. In the event of wet weather, the Drill Hall and St. Mary's Schools will be utilised for this purpose.

His Worship the Mayor desires to make a general appeal to the public of Barnsley to co-operate in the welcome to the men by displaying flags and bunting, especially along the line of route, and by their presence on Market Hill on Thursday morning. There should be a tremendous crowd to witness what will be a memorable and historic gathering.

The accommodation of St. Mary's Church is, of course, limited, and such members of the general public who desire to be present at the service must take their seats before 11.45 a.m.

The feeding of the men will be in the capable hands of the Barnsley British Co-operative Society, and the liquid refreshments will be given by the two local breweries—the Barnsley Brewery and Clarkson's Old Brewery Companies. The arrangements for the distribution of the refreshments is in the hands of a sub-committee consisting of ex-Company Sergt.-Majors Bridge, Morrison, Taylor, and Townend and Councillor W. Barnes.

The general arrangements in connection with the visit will be carried out by the Raising Committee of the Council, of which the Mayor is chairman, and they will have the assistance of Col. Sir Joseph Hewitt, Col. T. W. H. Mitchell, and Col Fox. The provision of a band has kindly been arranged for by Col. Fox.

The line of route from the Queen's Grounds will be: Queen's Road, Kendray Street, Eldon Street, and Market Hill.

The strength of the cadre will be 50 men and 5 officers. It is interesting to note that Major Goodburn, the present Commanding Officer of the 13th Battalion, joined the Second Barnsley Battalion as a Second-Lieutenant on its formation early in 1914, and he has been with one or other of the Battalions throughout the war. The officers of the cadre will be the guests of the Mayor at luncheon at the Queen's Hotel on Thursday at the conclusion of the ceremony at the Church.

Whilst the cadre which will arrive in the town on Wednesday will be that of the 13th Battalion, it will in reality represent both the local Battalions which were raised for Kitchener's Army in the early days of the great war. When the Division in which the Battalions were was re-organised, the 14th was partly merged into the 13th and partly into another Service Battalion of the York and Lancaster Regiment, and there is no longer a 14th Battalion. The Colours to be handed over into safe keeping in St. Mary's Church, are, of course, the actual colours of the 13th Battalion, but the merging of the two Battalions is the reason why the discharged and demobilised men of both Battalions will parade on Thursday.

In order to prevent any misunderstanding, the Mayor wishes it to be distinctly understood that the welcome to the Colour party is quite a separate function from the welcome to be given to the whole of the Barnsley men who have served. This will take place at a later date, when there will be an assembly of all service men for a civic welcome home.

APPEAL TO ALL OLD 'PALS.'

BIG MUSTER WANTED.

The Barnsley Branch of the National Federation of Discharged and Disabled Sailors and Soldiers makes a special appeal to all its members who were originally either with the 13th or 14th Battalions to participate in the reception, and to parade at the Queen's Grounds on Thursday morning. In view of the fact that the inspection takes place at 10.30, the men are urgently requested to be there not later than 10 o'clock.

Uniform may be put on if desired, and a request is made that medals and decorations shall be worn.

All ex-officers, warrant officers and N.C.O.'s are invited to meet at 10, Peel Street, on Wednesday evening, at 7 o'clock, to discuss arrangements concerning Thursday morning's parade.

The civic welcome home to all Barnsley service men, to take place at a later date, will include sailors and soldiers from many regiments. Thursday's ceremony is the Barnsley Pals' Battalion's own particular day, and it is doubtful whether there will be another such opportunity for them to march shoulder to shoulder in Peace as they did in War.

A big muster of "Pals" is required. The authorities want it, and the people want it, and we trust the response to the appeal will be most gratifying.

If you served with the 13th or 14th Battalions, don't be satisfied to look on, but be on parade.

THE OFFICIAL PROGRAMME.

BARNSLEY COUNTY BOROUGH COUNCIL.

NOTICE.

THE CADRE OF THE 13th BATTALION, YORK & LANCASTER REGIMENT WILL RETURN TO THE TOWN FOR THE PURPOSE OF

DEPOSITING THE KING'S COLOURS IN THE PARISH CHURCH, ON THURSDAY, MAY 29, 1919.

All Officers and Men of the 13th and 14th Battalions, York and Lancaster Regiment, are cordially invited to attend and take part in the proceedings.

THE PROGRAMME IN CONNECTION WITH THE VISIT WILL BE AS FOLLOWS:

Thursday 10 to 10-30 a.m.

The demobilised men of the 13th and 14th Battalions, York and Lancaster Regiment, will assemble in the Queen's Grounds. Each Battalion will be inspected by its former Commanding Officer.

11 a.m.

The Cadre will proceed from the Drill Hall to the Queen's Grounds, and will head the march of the two Battalions from the Queen's Grounds to Market Hill.

11-30 a.m.

The Mayor and Town Council will receive the Cadre and the men of the two Battalions on Market Hill. The Mayor will address the Cadre and the Battalions.

11-45 a.m.

The two Battalions will march from Market Hill to the Church door, and will then line the route from Market Hill, forming a Guard of Honour for the Mayor and the Town Council and the Cadre.

12 noon.

The Cadre and the Mayor and the Town Council will arrive at St. Mary's Church.

12 noon to 12-30.

Service in St. Mary's Church and depositing of King's Colours. Members of the General Public desiring to attend the Service must take their seats in the Church before 11.45 a.m. The accommodation for the general public is extremely limited. All wounded men unable to walk are requested to take their seats in the Church before 11.45 a.m.

1 p.m.

Battalions will march back to the Queen's Grounds, where sandwiches, beer and mineral waters will be provided for all men taking part in the procession.

The General Public are requested to co-operate in the welcome to the Men by displaying Flags, and by their presence on the line of Route and Market Hill.

W. E. RALEY, Mayor.

PLACING OF COLOURS IN PARISH CHURCH

FORM OF SERVICE.

1. National Anthem (3 verses).
2. Te Deum.
3. Lesser Litany, and Prayers.
4. Hymn No. 437 (Ancient and Hymn Book).

4a. Last Post.

5. Receiving of Colours at the Al
6. Short Prayer.
7. Hymn No. 391 (Ancient and Hymn Book).
8. Pronouncement of Benediction.
9. Recessional Hymn.

VISITS TO GRAVES IN FRA

It is believed that by the end of military restrictions on travelling to will be removed, and already many are planning to visit the graves of so the late war zone. Tourist agencies ceiving letters of inquiry on the subj latest development is the establishmen officers of a travel bureau. The itine sists of a three days' visit to Fran Amiens as the headquarters. It is lent centre for the battlefields of France, and all parts of the Som within easy reach by motor-car. The make themselves responsible for the at Victoria, and accommodate him in the same afternoon. Next morning driven to the required destination— the grave of his fallen kinsman may private motor car, and accompanied officer guide. The return journey to is made in time for dinner, and the to England is made on the third toria being reached in the evening. charged for the visit will be for one guineas, two persons 30 guineas, th sons 40 guineas, four persons 50 guin persons 60 guineas. The visits ca tended beyond the three days at a mentary charge of two guineas per person for hotel accommodation and and 10 guineas per day for the use vate car for two or three persons, services of an officer guide. Should "rush" visit of two days from Lon return be desired, a car with an offic can be sent to meet the traveller or at Cailais or Boulogne. The bureau intending travellers that "the journe any means an excursion, but a vi to the graves, in a proper spirit, due reverence."

The number of soldiers' graves no fied and registered in France and Be 373,351. The number of other bur ported is 154,823. In many of these burials took place under such condit the graves were never found, and all markings have been destroyed b fire. During the last month 2,125 suc have been identified and registered, hoped a considerable number more traced. Some considerable time mu before all requests for photographs can and the present situation does not per general permission being given to visi Relatives are strongly advised that should be undertaken without first a ing from the Directorate of Graves tion and Inquiries, War Office, Wi House, St. James's Square, S.W.1, t grave is registered.

FOOD CONTROL OF THE FU

The possibility of the retention of trol in some of its forms was fores recently, and a well-informed corres says the Cabinet has just instructed cials of the Ministry of Food to prepa for presentation to Parliament this giving effect to certain recomme made by the Consumers' Council. will, it is said, include a provision tea, coffee, and cocoa must be sold weight.

COST OF BUILDING MATER

The Local Government Board iss following statement:—It has been br the attention of the President of th Government Board that the presen market prices of building materials a ing to deter, or to prejudice, the ra motion of State-aided housing schem he wishes it to be known that, by tion and large-scale buying, contracts supply of building material have been into by the Government which show able saving on the ruling market Local authorities and other promo State-aided housing schemes obtainin building materials from or throu Ministry of Supply, will be given the tage of this economy, which, though to express in a general figure, amo from 10 to 15 per cent. on present prices, and in some cases more. Ap should be sent to "The Director of Material Supplies, Ministry of Supp ton House Tothill Street, London, S

Printed and published by the "Chronicle," Limited, at their "Chronicle" Buildings, Peel Barnsley, in the West Riding County of York.

TUESDAY, MAY 27, 191

Thursday, 29 May 1919, 11.30am. Lieutenant- Colonel Hewitt addressing some of the surviving Barnsley Pals on Market Hill.

The Cadre march the precious Battle Honours into St Mary's Church.

**June 1919
28th**
The Treaty of Versailles was signed by the Germans.

Sources and Further Reading

Barnsley Chronicle: All issues consulted 1913-1919

The Times: various issues consulted between 1914-1919

The Great War 1914-1919: H. W. Wilson, published in 13 volumes as events occurred, Amalgamated Press Ltd.

The Macmillan Dictionary of The First World War, Stephen Pope and Elizabeth-Anne Wheal, Macmillan, 1995

A Companion To World War I, edited by John Horne, Blackwell Publishing Ltd, 2010

An Illustrated Companion To The First World War, Anthony Bruce, Michael Joseph, London 1989

The Long Shadow, David Reynolds, Simon & Shuster, 2013

The Great War 1914-1918, Peter Hart, Profile Books, 2014

Acknowledgements

Jane Ainsworth, Paul Ainsworth, Keith Atack, Vera Atack (1938–2017), Carole Mays Baird, Dr Gordon Mays Baird (1943-2016), Michael Barber, Susan Barber, Giles Brearley, Ruth Brearley, Jodie Butterwood, Vincent Carmichael, Jon Cooksey, Tyler Crellin, Robert A. Dale, Joanna C. Murray Deller, Aydan Deller, Ricky S. Deller, Tracy P. Deller, Brian Elliott, Dave Hayes, Charles Hewitt, Keith Hopkins, Keith Hopkinson, Gary (Jack) Foster, Ann Howse, Matt Jones, Heather Law, Amy Legg, Kevin McGovern, Susan McGovern, Brendan E. McNally, John D. Murray, Bill Peake, Barrie Stacey, Bogdan I Trandafir, Adam R. Walker, Anna Walker, Arthur O. Walker, Christine Walker, Darren J. Walker, David Walker, Emma C. Walker, Isaac Walker, Ivan P. Walker, Jenny Walker, Paula L. Walker, Polly Walker, Rose O. Walker, Suki B. Walker, Thomas Walker, Marie Webster, Margaret Willoughby, Jon Wilkinson, Paul Wilkinson, Roni Wilkinson and finally, not forgetting my ever-faithful walking companion, Coco.

Index